Insights You Need from
Harvard Business Review

MULTI
GENERATIONAL
WORKPLACE

Insights You Need from Harvard Business Review

Business is changing. Will you adapt or be left behind?

Get up to speed and deepen your understanding of the topics that are shaping your company's future with the **Insights You Need from Harvard Business Review** series. Featuring HBR's smartest thinking on fast-moving issues—blockchain, cybersecurity, AI, and more—each book provides the foundation introduction and practical case studies your organization needs to compete today and collects the best research, interviews, and analysis to get it ready for tomorrow.

You can't afford to ignore how these issues will transform the landscape of business and society. The Insights You Need series will help you grasp these critical ideas—and prepare you and your company for the future.

Books in the series includes:

Agile

Artificial Intelligence

Blockchain

Climate Change

Coronavirus: Leadership and Recovery

Crypto

Customer Data and Privacy

Cybersecurity

The Future of Work

Global Recession

Hybrid Workplace

Monopolies and Tech Giants

Multigenerational Workplace

Racial Justice

Strategic Analytics

Supply Chain

Web3

The Year in Tech, 2023

The Year in Tech 2024

Insights You Need from
Harvard Business Review

MULTI GENERATIONAL WORKPLACE

Harvard Business Review Press
Boston, Massachusetts

Copyright 2023 Harvard Business School Publishing Corporation
All rights reserved
Printed in the United States of America

10   9   8   7   6   5   4   3   2   1

No part of this publication may be reproduced, stored in or introduced into a retrieval system, or transmitted, in any form, or by any means (electronic, mechanical, photocopying, recording, or otherwise), without the prior permission of the publisher. Requests for permission should be directed to permissions@hbsp.harvard.edu, or mailed to Permissions, Harvard Business School Publishing, 60 Harvard Way, Boston, Massachusetts 02163.

The web addresses referenced in this book were live and correct at the time of the book's publication but may be subject to change.

Cataloging-in-Publication data is forthcoming.

ISBN: 978-1-64782-500-3
eISBN: 978-1-64782-501-0

The paper used in this publication meets the requirements of the American National Standard for Permanence of Paper for Publications and Documents in Libraries and Archives Z39.48-1992.

Contents

Contents

Section 2

Bridging Generational Divides

MULTI GENERATIONAL WORKPLACE

Introduction

HARNESSING THE POWER OF AGE DIVERSITY

by Megan W. Gerhardt, Josephine Nachemson-Ekwall, and Brandon Fogel

Conflict between generations is an age-old phenomenon. But at the end of 2019, when the retort "OK, Boomer" went viral, the vitriol—from both young people who said it and older people who opposed it—was pointed and widespread.

The sarcastic phrase was coined by a younger generation to push back on an older one that its members saw as dismissive and condescending, and it became popular from

Korea to New Zealand even though the term "Boomer" is barely used outside of the United States. The retort captured the yawning divide between the generations over seemingly every issue: political activism, climate change, social media, technology, privacy, gender identity.

With five generations together in U.S. workplaces for the first time (Silent Generation, Baby Boomers, Gen X, Millennials, and Gen Z), and similar dynamics playing out in other parts of the world, tensions are mounting. The anger and lack of trust they can cause hurt team performance by limiting collaboration, sparking emotional conflict, and leading to higher employee turnover and lower team performance. And a lack of awareness and understanding of age issues can drive discrimination in hiring and promotion, resulting in lawsuit risks.

But many organizations don't take steps to address generational issues. While companies have recently renewed their diversity efforts, only 8% of organizations include age as part of their DEI strategy.[1] And of organizations that do address it, the strategy has often been to simply encourage those of different generations to focus on their similarities or to deny the reality of their differences altogether.

This is a missed opportunity. Age-diverse teams are valuable because they bring together people with complementary abilities, skills, information, and networks.

If managed effectively, they can offer better decision-making, more-productive collaboration, and improved overall performance—but only if members are willing to share and learn from their differences. Think of a multigenerational team of product developers, merging the seasoned experience and broad client network of its older members with the fresh perspectives and up-to-date supplier network of its younger ones. Such a group can use its age diversity to build something no single generation could on its own.

Take the Open Sustainability Technology Lab at Michigan Technological University, a multigenerational team that developed the first low-cost open-source metal 3D printer.[2] Former director Joshua Pearce credits the team's success to members' willingness to learn from those of other generations. To develop their new product, they needed the technical skills of Gen X faculty, the software wizardry of Millennial graduate students, and the experienced resourcefulness of Boomer researchers. For example, when a younger team member turned to Amazon to order an urgently needed mechanical component, an older colleague intervened and built it from spare parts more quickly than even Amazon could have delivered it. By combining abilities, the team developed the ability to 3D print in aluminum and steel at a much lower cost than had been possible.

That's why papering over generational differences isn't the answer. Through our work with age-diverse groups in finance, health care, sports, agriculture, and R&D, we've found that a better approach is to help people acknowledge, appreciate, and make use of their differences—just as organizations do with other kinds of diversity. Evidence shows that when time-tested DEI tools are used to bridge age divides, they can reduce conflict and generational stereotypes and improve organizational commitment, job satisfaction, employee turnover, and organizational performance.[3]

In our book, *Gentelligence,* we lay out our framework for moving colleagues away from generational conflict and toward a productive embrace of one another's differences. There are four practices involved. The first two, *identify your assumptions* and *adjust your lens*, help overcome false stereotypes. The next two, *take advantage of differences* and *embrace mutual learning*, guide people to share knowledge and expertise so that they can grow together. Each practice also includes an activity to apply its ideas. Teams experiencing generational conflict should start with the first two; the latter two will help groups move beyond simply getting along and leverage the learning and innovation that intergenerational teams can offer.

To introduce the framework, let's look at what makes a generation—and what makes generations different from each other.

Generations Today

A generation is an age cohort whose members are born during the same period in history and who thus experience significant events and phenomena at similar life stages. These collective experiences—say, high unemployment, a population boom, or political change—can shape the group's values and norms in a unique way. Because these formative experiences vary from culture to culture, the specifics of generational makeup vary around the world.

But across geographies, the different outlooks, attitudes, and behaviors of cohorts can lead to conflict. For example, in many countries, older workers, who have dominated the workplace for decades, are staying in it longer due to better health and longevity. Younger colleagues, anxious for change and upward mobility, are often impatient for them to move on. And when Boomers and digital natives work side by side, tensions can arise about whose contributions are valued more. If the client

How Are Generations Defined?

In the United States there are currently five generations in the workforce: the Silent Generation (typically considered to have been born 1928–1945), Baby Boomers (1946–1964), Gen X (1965–1980), Millennials (1981–1996), and Gen Z (1997–2012).

Each experienced different world events as members came of age, which shaped their views on jobs and careers—and fueled the stereotypes that people have about them. For example, members of the Silent Generation had more prosperity in their adult years than their parents did; they earned a reputation for doing what was asked of them without complaint and building secure lives for their families. Boomers grew up amid economic growth and possibility, relishing long hours at the office and becoming known as workaholics. Gen Xers enjoyed more independence as children than prior generations, leading them to crave greater autonomy and balance in their careers, which then led to them being seen as slackers by their elders. And Millennials, whose development was actively nurtured by their parents from an early age, have come to be seen as expecting rapid career advancement.

Other parts of the world don't necessarily label generations this way; instead, specific age cohorts often acquire a name when their births or childhoods coincide with events of particular culture relevance. Examples include the "little emperors" of China, born during the country's one-child policy; the "born frees" of South Africa, who arrived after apartheid ended; and Kenya's Uhuru ("freedom") Generation, born after the country gained independence. In Sweden cohorts tend to be grouped by decade, but even that can spark tension. Notably, a politician stirred controversy in the early 2000s by coining the name *köttberg*, or "meat mountain," to describe workers born in the 1940s, whom he saw as limiting youth employment.

Around the world, those born recently (such as late Gen Zers and Generation Alpha in the United States) are being shaped by the Covid-19 pandemic.

database that an older employee developed is replaced by automated software suggested by a younger associate, the older employee may feel that their contribution is being minimized.

These generational frustrations have become even more pronounced during the pandemic. While older workers have more experience, the 35-and-under age groups, according to a recent survey of hiring managers, are seen as having the most relevant education and skills and the best cultural fit for open positions. Even as people flocked online during the pandemic, different generations tended to spend time on different platforms—older people scrolling Facebook, younger ones TikTok—deepening the digital divide. Gen Z employees, meanwhile, have worked remotely for most if not all of their professional lives, leaving many feeling disconnected from coworkers and undervalued by their older teammates. And older generations have adjusted to working from home better than expected, finding the flexibility energizing after a lifetime of long hours at the office.

Many of these tensions—and the media hype around them—have led to a further decline in trust between the generations. The steps we outline in the four practices and activities below are designed to help bridge that gap and move toward better intergenerational cooperation.

Identify Your Assumptions

The assumptions we make about generational groups (including our own) can hold us back from understanding teammates' true selves as well as the skills, information, and connections they have to offer. Noticing that we're making these assumptions is the first step to combating them.

Take headlines such as this one from 2019: "Why 'Lazy,' 'Entitled' Millennials Can't Last 90 Days at Work."[4] As is often the case, the stereotype on display falls apart on closer inspection. Pew Research Center has found that 70% of Millennials, who are currently aged 26 to 41, stick with their employers for at least 13 months; 69% of Gen Xers stayed that long during the same period of their lives.[5]

Not all biases are blatant enough to make headlines. But even beliefs that we hold at the subconscious level can influence our interactions and our decision-making, often without us realizing it. For example, imagine being asked to nominate a few teammates to lead an Instagram campaign. Who comes to mind? Probably some of your 20-something colleagues. Consciously, you may believe you are choosing those who are the most qualified, most interested, and most able to benefit from the experience. Unconsciously, you may be falling back on deeply embedded assumptions that older people dislike technology or are uninterested in learning anything new.

When it comes to conflict on intergenerational teams, people often rightly suspect there's something age-related going on, but they frequently assume it means something other than what it really does. Let's look at how this played out on one team we studied. At the Fung Fellowship at the University of California, Berkeley, leaders created teams of undergraduates and retirees to collaborate on wellness products for older adults. Initially, these teams ran into several interpersonal challenges. For example, when the retirees didn't respond quickly to texts sent by their younger peers, the students felt that their counterparts weren't taking them or the project seriously. Meanwhile, the retirees resented their teammates' assumptions and seemingly haphazard communication. Work slowed as relations became strained.

Such teams need a tool to recognize the specific age biases they may hold, understand tensions that exist, and head off brewing conflict. We recommend an assumption audit.

Activity: Assumption Audit

Challenge employees to spend a week on high alert for age-based assumptions in their daily work. Have them pay attention to their own actions as well as others'. This might mean noticing, for example, that a team leader dismissed a young employee's request for more responsibility as "entitled" behavior or that you left senior employees out of your meeting on innovation.

After the week has passed, schedule time with the group to discuss its experiences, asking each person to bring at least one observation to the table. These conversations can get charged or lead to defensiveness, but clear ground rules can go a long way in preventing those outcomes. Instruct people to speak about what they heard and saw but not to assume intent: "Input from our younger teammates is dismissed quickly" rather than "Senior leaders dismiss our younger teammates' input because they don't think they have anything to offer." Encourage everyone to be open to feedback and to consider how age-based assumptions—whether containing some truth or absolutely false—might be affecting team cohesion, engagement, and performance.

Plan a follow-up meeting for several weeks later to continue the conversation, ensure accountability, and start building awareness into your everyday work.

When the Fung Fellowship program leaders did their own assumption audit to uncover why the undergraduate-retiree teams were struggling, they found that younger team members had assumed that texts sent after hours would be deemed urgent and would get a quick reply. But older peers thought it went without saying that a text could wait until morning. Identifying these assumptions prompted the team to set shared norms around communication.

Adjust Your Lens

Recognizing assumptions is important, but teams also need to combat them. Stereotypes often cause us to incorrectly attribute differences to age or to assume ill intent where there is none. *Adjusting your lens* means considering whether the assumptions that you've identified align with the reality of the situation at hand, or whether you've been judging someone's actions and attitudes based only on your frame of reference. Try to understand *why* colleagues from different generations might behave differently than you do. To expand your thinking in that way, use the describe-interpret-evaluate exercise.

Activity: Describe-Interpret-Evaluate Exercise

Developed in the 1970s to prepare employees to work abroad, this exercise can also help members of age-diverse teams broaden their understanding of one another.

First, have each employee *describe* a frustration they have with someone of a different generation. Next, ask them to think about their initial *interpretation* of the person's behavior. Finally, challenge them to come up with an alternative *evaluation* of your interpretation; they can also ask for contributions from the group.

For example, recently one of us (Megan) conducted a workshop with a group of health care professionals. A nursing manager who identified herself as a Baby Boomer described being annoyed with young patients who used their mobile phones in the middle of a conversation with a nurse or a doctor. Her interpretation was that the patients were—rudely—not paying attention to their caregiving team. When prompted to think of alternative explanations, she looked confused, unable to come up with anything. But her colleagues—mostly younger doctors and nurses—had plenty of ideas: The young patients might be taking notes on the conversation or looking up the pharmacy's hours to make sure they could get their prescriptions before closing. As her teammates offered these insights, the nursing manager's expression changed. She was able to see the behavior in a different light and better appreciate the patients' perspectives. At the same time, her younger colleagues realized how behavior that felt natural to them—like checking a phone mid-conversation—might offend older peers.

Take Advantage of Differences

Once you've tempered generational tensions by recognizing assumptions and adjusting lenses, you can work on finding productive differences with your colleagues of other generations and ways to benefit from each other's perspectives, knowledge, and networks.

For team members to feel comfortable sharing in this way—bringing up new ideas or conflicting information—they need to feel a certain amount of psychological safety, as the research of Harvard Business School's Amy Edmondson shows.[6] But, as we've seen, perceived generational competition in the workplace, exacerbated by clickbait headlines, has undermined trust. One good way to rebuild it is to hold a roundtable where the team's diverse perspectives can be acknowledged and valued.

Activity: Intergenerational Roundtable

Leaders of intergenerational teams should set monthly or quarterly meetings to elicit ideas for how to work together more productively and smoothly. There are two stages to the process:

1. **Find common ground and similarities.** While it may seem counterintuitive to focus on commonalities when the goal is to leverage differences, team members must first see themselves as collaborators on a joint mission, rather than competitors. Furthermore, research shows that having a common purpose and goals are vital to team performance.[7] Intergenerational teams can struggle more than most to find that shared ground. So at your first roundtable, ask teammates to work together to answer questions such as "Why does the team exist?" and "What shared goals do we want to accomplish?" This helps team members begin to see themselves as unified in pursuit of the same interests and builds psychological safety. At future sessions, remind team members of these discussions.

2. **Invite unique viewpoints.** Next, have each team member respond to the following questions:

   - What are we, as a team, doing well to accomplish these shared goals?

   - What are we doing that is keeping us from reaching these goals?

– What opportunities should we take advantage of that we currently aren't?

– If you were in charge, what would you continue, stop, or start doing?

Your aim is not to come to neat conclusions but to bring to light new ideas that might have been dismissed or unvoiced in the past. Different views will inevitably surface, and some conflict may even erupt—that's all right. Just keep steering the conversation back to the team's shared goals and emphasize that differences of opinion are valued contributions toward your common success.

Aaron Hornbrook, a customer service manager and vice president at Wells Fargo we've interviewed, holds monthly roundtable meetings with his multigenerational team. At the beginning of each, Hornbrook reminds everyone that their mission is to help customers with their application- and account-related questions and that success will require both trust and willingness to listen to the perspectives of the entire group. His efforts have borne fruit: For example, his Millennial and Gen Z employees feel comfortable voicing their concerns about mental health in the workplace—a subject that had been taboo in the workplace for much of their older colleagues' careers. These conversations helped Hornbrook and other senior colleagues understand why paid-time-off requests had spiked recently and prompted them to find ways to reduce employee anxiety, including by requiring supervisors to hold one-on-one meetings with direct reports in conference rooms rather than at their desks. As a result, team members of all generations became more supportive of people taking mental health days.

By creating a space for team members to discuss how the group functions, managers demonstrate that all perspectives are valued.

Embrace Mutual Learning

Finally, to fully reap the benefits of intergenerational teams, members must believe that they have something to learn from colleagues in different age cohorts. The ultimate goal is mutual learning: peers of all ages teaching and learning from one another in an ongoing loop.

One way to encourage this is with formal mentoring initiatives. While traditional mentoring programs (older colleagues teaching younger ones) exist at many organizations, a number of top companies—including GE, Deloitte, PwC, Cisco, and Procter & Gamble—have developed "reverse mentoring" programs, where younger people teach older peers new skills, typically around technology. We suggest that companies and even managers of small teams combine both approaches into two-way "mutual mentoring." Research shows that such programs support employees' development of competencies and skills and increase both individual involvement and collective motivation.[8]

Mutual learning can also happen organically when people of different generations have good relationships and are on the lookout for opportunities. BuildWitt Media, a digital storytelling firm we've studied, helps its clients in the construction and mining industries attract great talent. Its founder and CEO is 26-year-old Aaron Witt; its president, Dan Briscoe, is 53. While cross-generational learning was never an explicit reason for their partnership, they have come to value how Briscoe's 30 years of experience in leadership, sales, and marketing complement Witt's impulsive energy, sense of business trends, and lifelong immersion in mobile media. For example, Briscoe credits Witt with teaching him to look beyond academic degrees and GPA when hiring and to consider leadership potential and alignment with culture and values in addition to a work portfolio. Witt says Briscoe is good at relating to clients and putting deals together. This partnership, they agree, has led to rapid growth and the opportunity to diversify their services.

Activity: Mutual Mentoring

To start building a mentorship culture on your team, create an informal mutual mentoring network. Begin by asking team members of all ages what they want to learn and what they want to teach. Potential teachers can be surprisingly shy when it comes to their expertise; it may help if you make suggestions about what you see as their strengths.

Identify where there are natural connections: employees who are versed in TikTok and those who want to learn to create selfie videos, or employees who have an established roster of clients and those who want to expand their networks. While not all pairings need to be cross-generational, make sure all generations are represented in both the learner and the instructor groups.

Once you have some pairings ready, hold a kickoff meeting with the entire team and ask four to six mentors to present briefly on their area of expertise. Encourage people to reach out to the mentors whose skills they want to learn. Often the energy of the meeting itself will spur connections, but you can also send monthly nudges to remind the team to keep questions flowing.

Even this kind of informal network can help to build a culture of cross-generational learning.

. . .

"OK, Boomer," "Gen X cynics," "entitled Millennials," and "Gen Z snowflakes." We have become so entrenched in generational name-calling—or, conversely, so focused on downplaying the differences that do exist—that we have forgotten there is strength in age diversity. Especially at a time when we are wrestling with so many changes to the way we work, it's incumbent on leaders to embrace intergenerational teams as a key piece of the DEI puzzle and to frame them as an opportunity to be seized rather than a threat to be managed.

TAKEAWAYS

Lack of trust between workers of older and younger generations often yields a culture of competition and resentment. But when age-diverse teams are managed well, colleagues of all ages can share a wide array of skills, knowledge, and networks with one another. Tools that have been used successfully by cross-cultural teams for decades (and more recently, for DEI initiatives) can be applied to multi-generational teams. Four practices are recommended:

- ✓ **Identifying assumptions.** The Assumption Audit tool helps teams recognize the age biases they may hold, understand tensions that exist, and head off brewing conflict.

- ✓ **Adjusting your lens.** The Describe-Interpret-Evaluate exercise helps colleagues from different generations understand why they might think and behave differently.

- ✓ **Taking advantage of differences.** An Intergenerational Roundtable activity offers a space for team members to discuss how the group functions and for managers to demonstrate that all perspectives are valued.

- ✓ **Embracing mutual learning.** Mutual mentoring helps build a culture of cross-generational learning.

NOTES

1. SHRM Foundation, "Leveraging the Value of an Age-Diverse Workforce," n.d., https://www.shrm.org/foundation/ourwork

/initiatives/the-aging-workforce/Documents/Age-Diverse%20
Workforce%20Executive%20Briefing.pdf.

2. Gerald C. Anzalone et al., "A Low-Cost Open-Source Metal
3-D Printer," *IEEE Access* 1 (2013): 803–810.

3. Carol T. Kulik, Elissa L. Perry, and Anne C. Bourhis, "Ironic
Evaluation Processes: Effects of Thought Suppression on Evalua-
tions of Older Job Applicants," *Journal of Organizational Behavior*
21, no. 6 (2000): 689–711; Franziska Jungmann et al., "Improving
Team Functioning and Performance in Age-Diverse Teams: Evaluation of a Leadership Training," *Work, Aging, and Retirement* 6,
no. 3 (July 2020): 175–194.

4. Frank Chung, "Why 'Lazy,' 'Entitled' Millennials Can't Last 90
Days at Work," *New York Post*, March 12, 2019, https://nypost.com
/2019/03/12/why-lazy-entitled-millennials-cant-last-90-days-at
-work/.

5. Kristen Bialek and Richard Fry, "Millennial Life: How Young
Adulthood Today Compares with Prior Generations," Pew Research Center, Washington, DC, February 14, 2019, https://www
.pewresearch.org/social-trends/2019/02/14/millennial-life-how
-young-adulthood-today-compares-with-prior-generations-2/.

6. Amy Edmondson, "Psychological Safety and Learning Behavior
in Work Teams," *Administrative Science Quarterly* 44, no. 2 (1999):
350–383.

7. Annett Schöttle and Patricia A. Tillmann, "Explaining the
Benefits of Team Goals to Support Collaboration," in *Proceedings
of the 26th Annual Conference of the International Group for
Lean Construction (IGLC), Chennai, India, July 16–22, 2018, Vol. 1*,
ed. Vicente A. González (Chennai, India: IIT Madras, 2018):
432–441.

8. Jung H. Yun, Brian Baldi, and Mary Deane Sorcinelli, "Mutual Mentoring for Early-Career and Underrepresented Faculty: Model, Research, and Practice," *Innovative Higher Education* 41 (2016): 441–451.

Adapted from content posted on hbr.org, March 8, 2022 (product #H06WA9).

Section 1

UNDERSTANDING YOUR FIVE-GENERATION WORKFORCE

1

I WAS A MANAGER IN AN AGEIST WORKPLACE

by Nicole D. Smith

A few years back, I decided to chat with one of my team members, a man in his late fifties. I had recently started a new position as a manager—was just a few weeks on the job—and I wanted to see how people were adjusting to the change.

We found a quiet room and started discussing weekend plans and work projects. As the conversation continued, I found a moment to bring up an idea I'd been thinking about.

"OK," my employee replied, slightly suspicious yet curious. During my short time leading the team, I'd learned he was admired for both his talent and his tenure. So, getting his buy-in could mean others would be open to my idea.

"I think we should get together with the digital team and learn more about what they do," I said. "They seem to be smart and innovative. I think they could really help our work and take us to the next level."

He was silent, which made me a little uncomfortable. But I pressed on, explaining what the collaboration could mean—like learning new tools and fostering the support of a creative, visible group. As I outlined my vision of partnering with coworkers who were mostly in their twenties, he was less than enthusiastic. In fact, for a moment I thought I saw worry in his eyes.

After what seemed like forever, he awkwardly shifted his body. "You're not going to force us to work with *them*, are you?"

This was the first of numerous concerning conversations I had over the next several days. I discovered that most of my team members—people in their fifties and sixties, many cherished contributors to our organization—had no desire to work with "those young people on the other side of the room."

I also learned I was in a culture that normalized ageist behavior—one where making surface-level assumptions about younger colleagues was acceptable. And it went both ways: Younger employees often disparaged older colleagues' technical skills and willingness to learn. They lamented, publicly and privately, that their knowledge, insight, and skills weren't appreciated and that they were being obstructed from developing and advancing.

After I required my team to work on projects with younger coworkers, eventually they began to collaborate with the digital team openly and often. But this was the first time I'd worked in an organization where people perceived each other's value, to some degree, in terms of their age rather than their contribution, commitment, and potential.

After this experience and several others, I continued to wonder about ageism and how it affects the workplace. And I haven't stopped asking questions: How do we define and identify ageism at work? What can managers do about it? And what are the potential consequences if they do nothing?

What Ageism Is

At its core, ageism is discrimination based on age. In the United States, the Age Discrimination in Employment

Act forbids it against people who are 40 or older. The World Health Organization (WHO) divides ageism into several layers: how we think (stereotypes), how we feel (prejudices), and how we act toward others or even ourselves (discrimination) because of age. Taken together, the WHO reports, those types of behaviors can affect physical and mental health and can even shorten people's lives by up to seven and a half years.

Researcher Justyna Stypińska and sociologist Konrad Turek conducted an extensive study that shows ageist behaviors at work can take two forms: *hard* and *soft*.[1] Hard age discrimination is illegal or prohibited behaviors, such as firing, demoting, or severely harassing someone because of age. Soft discrimination, like an off-color joke or comment, isn't necessarily illegal and mostly occurs in interpersonal interactions. The soft form is the more common one, and women experience it more often than men. Since soft discrimination is mostly rooted in stereotypes, it can lead to people not valuing coworkers' contribution and perspectives and even negatively assessing their skill sets.

The primary victims of ageist work cultures tend to be at the poles—the youngest and oldest workers. Members of the first group are seen as inexperienced and having less to offer, which can make it difficult for them to find employment or negotiate with hiring managers for fair wages. Meanwhile, studies show older people struggle to get promotions, find new work, and change careers; this is particularly true for women and minority racial groups in the United States.[2] When ageism is rampant, older workers might be seen not only in a negative light but also as lower status than even very young peers, despite having lower turnover and high-rated job performance.

People often equate generation with age. But when I talked to Peter Cappelli, a professor at the Wharton School of the University of Pennsylvania, he told me age and generation are not exactly the same. A generation is created when people experience something so distinctive and powerful that it leaves a unique impression on you and your cohort. Age has more to do with life stages, such as starting a career, having children, or preparing for retirement.

In the workplace ageism can be insidious and pervasive and can have a negative influence across groups. It can dissolve solidarity, limit the contributions of younger and older employees alike, and lead to people being devalued and excluded. Experts say that if managers allow ageist behaviors to persist, employee job satisfaction, engagement, and commitment all decline.

How to Identify Ageism at Work

According to Cappelli, ageism surfaces in different ways, starting with hiring.

"You can see it in the recruiting side," he told me, even in job descriptions and interviews. There are key words typically associated with youth, such as *new ideas* and *fresh perspective*, as well as more positive ways of saying "older," like *experienced*. If hiring managers require an applicant to list a grade point average, consciously or not they're targeting people in a certain stage of life—typically those within a few years of graduation. Look, too, at how the company presents itself through pictures on its website, marketing materials, and events. "If all you see are really young people, that tells you something," Cappelli said.

Ageism also appears in HR practices and management decisions: promotions, terminations, training, leadership development, and project assignments. The types of employees who are groomed for and elevated to important roles may convey messages about age. Is it the case, for instance, that younger workers get all the promotions for digital-focused jobs?

Cappelli says that even office activities can be red flags. Offering foosball tournaments and unlimited beer after hours, for example, may attract workers of some age groups and not others.

To help identify ageism, managers can collect data. Qualitative data from one-on-one, informal conversations with employees can help unearth concerns that might have gone unnoticed. "Stay interviews" provide insight into how people feel before they decide to leave or retire. Remember to ask open-ended questions like *What can I do to support you?* and *What motivates (or demotivates) you?*

You can also use more-formal methods, such as employee surveys, to collect quantitative data. And look for age patterns in HR's people analytics about who goes and who stays.

Combating Ageism at Work

To combat ageism, Cappelli encourages managers to start with something simple, like how the company depicts employees visually. For example, ensure that in-office and public-facing images include people of all age groups.

The harder work is in changing behaviors: what people say, do, encourage, and accept. It all comes down to understanding. Lindsey Pollak, author of *The Remix: How to Lead and Succeed in the Multigenerational Workplace,* says managers can ignite change by creating multigenerational committees and seating arrangements. "What you tend to see in an office is all the executives of one age sit in one place, all the young people are in the bullpen, and all the middle managers are elsewhere. And I think that should be abolished." She also says managers must be deliberate in getting to know employees of all ages—and getting them to know one another.

Leaders don't have to let ageism quietly simmer, either. To spark change, start with language. Consider the comments, jokes, or labels people use to describe younger and older employees and whether they are microaggressions or are biased or insensitive. Overt terms, such as "old-timer" and "youngster," should be eradicated, as should euphemisms like "seasoned" and "newbie." Needless references to someone's age set the stage for conflict. Think, too, about what your work culture values. Studies show organizations commonly use reward systems to shape norms. In your company, are managers who hire up-and-comers as celebrated as those who recruit established stars? Do leaders equally laud the skills of digital natives and the institutional knowledge of older workers? Both are needed for an organization to thrive.

Younger workers (and hiring managers of all ages) should be encouraged to think about the assets that older workers bring to the table: experience, social skills, the ability to work independently. Similarly, older workers should understand what younger peers can offer, such as being tech savvy and valuing diversity.

Finally, recruiting strategies should yield a diverse group of people, including older and younger candidates. Advertise with organizations that have members 55 and older as well as on job boards for college students and other relevant, frequently visited employment sites.

What I Learned

I still think about when I wanted to bring that group of older employees together with the younger digital team.

As a manager, I had to understand how ageist ideas were affecting our work—and then be brave enough to change the culture and create an environment where everyone, however young or old, felt comfortable. Knowing this problem wasn't something I could tackle on my own, I asked other managers to have their teams work on projects with my direct reports; to set a good example, we got in the trenches with them on those collaborations.

I also built a mixed-age team by hiring people over 60, under 30, and all ages in between; helping young and older workers see their ideas through and become more visible in the organization, offering training in new technologies to my team members, and promoting one of my oldest employees.

Despite the initial apprehension, my team and several others in the office eventually learned to work together without worrying about age. Through the years, we became more inclusive and creative. We challenged the status quo, and in some ways, we became the personification of the adage "As iron sharpens iron, so one person sharpens another." Our differences helped us learn, and we made each other better.

Today, I challenge managers in my professional network to see the value in mixed-age teams. And I'm asking you to help all employees—from recent college graduates to those nearing retirement—see how pivotal their contributions are to your outcomes and organization.

TAKEAWAYS

Ageism is prevalent in the workplace. It can begin with who is recruited and hired and may continue through promotions, terminations, training, leadership development, and project assignments. Leaders can use the following strategies to recognize ageism and make their organizations more age-inclusive, equitable, and supportive.

✓ Managers should collect data on ageism and identify patterns about retention and turnover among different generations. Qualitative data (conversations with employees) and quantitative data (employee surveys) should be considered.

✓ Younger and older workers should be encouraged to think about the assets that other age cohorts bring.

✓ Companies should consider how they depict employees visually in their communications. Ensure that in-office and public-facing images include people of all age groups.

✓ Leaders should model the use of nonageist language. Think about the comments, jokes, or labels people use to describe younger and older employees and whether they are biased or insensitive.

✓ Consider whether your recruiting strategies are yielding an age-diverse range of candidates.

NOTES

1. Justyna Stypińska and Konrad Turek, "Hard and Soft Age Discrimination: The Dual Nature of Workplace Discrimination," *European Journal of Ageing* 14 (2017): 49–61.

2. David M. Cadiz, Amy C. Pytlovany, and Donald M. Truxillo, "Ageism in the Workplace," *Organizational and Institutional Psychology*, March 17, 2019, https://oxfordre.com/psychology/view/10.1093/acrefore/9780190236557.001.0001/acrefore-9780190236557-e-2.

Adapted from content posted on hbr.org, March 8, 2022 (product #H06WHG).

BUILD YOUR
LONGEVITY STRATEGY

by Paul Irving

Before our eyes, the world is undergoing a massive demographic transformation. In many countries, the population is getting old. Very old. Globally, the number of people aged 60 and over is projected to double to more than two billion by 2050, and those 60 and over will outnumber children under the age of five. In the United States, about 10,000 people turn 65 each day, and one in five Americans will be 65 or older by 2030. By 2035, Americans of retirement age will eclipse the number of people aged 18 and under for the first time in U.S. history.

The reasons for this age shift are many—medical advances that keep people healthier longer, dropping fertility rates, and so on—but the net result is the same: Populations around the world will look very different in the decades ahead.

Some in the public and private sector are already taking note—and sounding the alarm. In his first term as chairman of the U.S. Federal Reserve, with the Great Recession looming, Ben Bernanke remarked, "In the coming decades, many forces will shape our economy and our society, but in all likelihood no single factor will have as pervasive an effect as the aging of our population." Back in 2010, Standard & Poor's predicted that the biggest influence on "the future of national economic health, public finances, and policymaking" will be "the irreversible rate at which the world's population is aging."

This societal shift will undoubtedly change work, too: More and more Americans want to work longer—or have to, given that many aren't saving adequately for retirement. Soon, the workforce will include people from as many as five generations ranging in age from teenagers to 80-somethings.

Are companies prepared? The short answer is "no." Aging will affect every aspect of business operations—whether it's talent recruitment, the structure of compensation and benefits, the development of products

FIGURE 2-1

The world is getting older

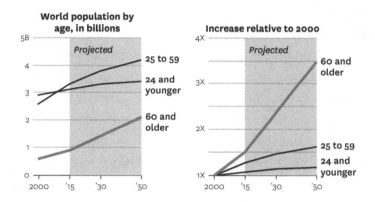

World population by
age, in billions

Increase relative to 2000

Source: United Nations, Department of Economic and Social Affairs, "World Population Prospects: 2015 Revision," July 29, 2015, https://www.un.org/en/development/desa/publications/world-population-prospects-2015-revision.html.

and services, how innovation is unlocked, how offices and factories are designed, and even how work is structured—but for some reason, the message just hasn't gotten through. In general, corporate leaders have yet to invest the time and resources necessary to fully grasp the unprecedented ways that aging will change the rules of the game.

What's more, those who *do* think about the impacts of an aging population typically see a looming crisis—not an opportunity. They fail to appreciate the potential that older adults present as workers and consumers. The reality, however, is that increasing longevity contributes to global economic growth. Today's older adults are generally healthier and more active than those of generations past, and they are changing the nature of retirement as they continue to learn, work, and contribute. In the workplace, they provide emotional stability, complex problem-solving skills, nuanced thinking, and institutional know-how. Their talents complement those of younger workers, and their guidance and support enhance performance and intergenerational collaboration. In encore careers, volunteering, and civic and social settings, their experience and problem-solving abilities contribute to society's well-being.

In the public sector, policy makers are beginning to take action. Efforts are under way in the United States to reimagine communities to enhance "age friendliness," develop strategies to improve infrastructure, enhance wellness and disease prevention, and design new ways to invest for retirement as traditional income sources like pensions and defined benefit plans dry up. But such efforts are still early stage, and, given the slow pace of governmental change, they will likely take years to evolve.

Companies, by contrast, are uniquely positioned to change practices and attitudes *now*. Transformation won't be easy, but companies that move past today's preconceptions about older employees and respond and adapt to changing demographics will realize significant dividends, generating new possibilities for financial return and enhancing the lives of their employees and customers. I spent many years in executive management, corporate law, and board service. Based on this experience, along with research conducted with Arielle Burstein, Kevin Proff, and other members of our staff at the Milken Institute Center for the Future of Aging, I have developed a framework for building a "longevity strategy" that companies can use to create a vibrant multigenerational workforce. Broadly, a longevity strategy should include two key elements: internal-facing activities (hiring, retention, and mining the talents of workers of all ages) and external-facing ones (how your company positions itself and its products and services to customers and stakeholders). In this article, I'll address the internal activities companies should be engaging in.

First, let's examine why leaders seem to be overlooking the opportunities of an aging population.

The Ageism Effect

There's broad consensus that the global population is changing and growing significantly older. There's also a prevailing opinion that the impacts on society will largely be negative. A Government Accountability Office report warns that older populations will bring slower growth, lower productivity, and increasing dependency on society. A report from the Congressional Budget Office projects that higher entitlement costs associated with an aging population will drive up expenses relative to revenues, increasing the federal deficit. The World Bank foresees fading potential in economies across the globe, warning in 2018 of "headwinds from ageing populations in both advanced and developing economies, expecting decreased labor supply and productivity growth." Such predictions serve to further entrench the belief that older workers are an expensive drag on society.

What's at the heart of this gloomy outlook? Economists often refer to what's known as the dependency ratio: the number of people not typically in the workforce—those younger than 15 and older than 65—in a population divided by the number of working-age people. This measure assumes that older adults are generally unproductive and can be expected to do little other than consume benefits in their later years. Serious concerns about the so-called silver tsunami are justified if this assumption is correct: The prospect of a massive population of sick, disengaged, lonely, needy, and cognitively impaired people is a dark one indeed.

FIGURE 2-2

The global aging phenomenon

Projected breakdown of world population, by region

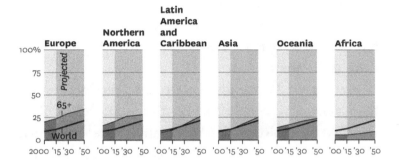

Source: United Nations, Department of Economic and Social Affairs, "World Population Prospects: 2015 Revision," July 29, 2015, https://www.un.org/en/development/desa /publications/world-population-prospects-2015-revision.html.

Northern America consists of Canada and the United States.

This picture, however, is simply not accurate. While some older adults do suffer from disabling physical and cognitive conditions or are otherwise unable to maintain an active lifestyle, far more are able and inclined to stay in the game longer, disproving assumptions about their prospects for work and productivity. The work of Laura Carstensen and her colleagues at the Stanford Center on Longevity shows that typical 60-something workers today are healthy, experienced, and more likely than younger colleagues to be satisfied with their jobs. They have a strong work ethic and loyalty to their employers. They are motivated, knowledgeable, adept at resolving social dilemmas, and care more about meaningful contributions and less about self-advancement. They are more likely than their younger counterparts to build social cohesion and to share information and organizational values.

Yet the flawed perceptions persist, a by-product of stubborn and pervasive ageism. Positive attributes of older workers are crowded out by negative stereotypes that infect work settings and devalue older adults in a youth-oriented culture. Older adults regularly find themselves on the losing end of hiring decisions, promotions, and even volunteer opportunities. Research from AARP found that approximately two-thirds of workers ages 45 to 74 said they have seen or experienced age discrimination in the workplace.[1] Of those, a remarkable 92% said age discrimination is very, or somewhat, common. Research for the Federal Reserve Bank of San Francisco backs this up. A study involving 40,000 made-up résumés found compelling evidence that older applicants, especially women, suffer consistent age discrimination.[2]

There's more: Deloitte's study *2018 Global Human Capital Trends* found that 20% of business and HR leaders surveyed viewed older workers as a competitive disadvantage and an impediment to the progress of younger workers.[3] The report concludes that "there may be a significant hidden problem of age bias in the workforce today." It also warns: "Left unaddressed, perceptions that a company's culture and employment practices suffer from age bias could damage its brand and social capital."

The negative cultural overlay about aging is reinforced by media and advertising that often portray older adults in clichéd, patronizing ways. A classic example is Life Alert's ad from the 1980s for its medical alert necklace, immortalizing the phrase "I've fallen, and I can't get up!" Recent ads by E*TRADE and Postmates have also drawn criticism as ageist. A more subtle but just as damaging example is the trumpeting of "antiaging" benefits on beauty products as a marketing tool, suggesting that growing older is, by definition, a negative process.

Some companies are pushing back: In a 2017 video, T-Mobile's John Legere took on the topic of ageist stereotypes while promoting a T-Mobile service for adults aged 55-plus.[4] He chided competitors for what he called their belittling treatment of older adults in marketing campaigns that emphasize large-size phone buttons and imply that Baby Boomers are tech idiots. "Degrading at the highest level," Legere calls it. "The carriers assume Boomers are a bunch of old people stuck in the past who

The Global Population Is Aging. Is Your Business Prepared?

by Jennifer D. Sciubba

It's important to recognize that our common assumptions around different countries' demographic makeups may be out of date. At the turn of the century, countries such as Japan, Italy, and Germany were among the world's oldest populations—but today, Thailand and Cuba are just as old, with Iran, Kuwait, Vietnam, and Chile close behind. In a decade, we can expect smaller cohorts of young people in these countries to begin to enter the market as workers and as customers, thus increasing the average age of these populations.

These are critical considerations when identifying new markets for investment. Different countries will respond differently to these shifts, and business leaders would be

can't figure out how the internet works. News flash, carriers: Boomers invented the internet."

Yet for the most part, employers continue to invest far more in young employees and generally do not train workers over 50. In fact, many companies would rather not think wise to pay attention not just to the demographic trends of a given market, but to how its leaders are likely to react to them. With more and more elders to care for, will governments take on the financial responsibility? Or will companies or individuals be expected to bear the burden? A country's approach to managing its aging population can influence its potential as a talent pool or customer base in substantial and nuanced ways.

Jennifer D. Sciubba is the author of *8 Billion and Counting: How Sex, Death, and Migration Shape Our World* and a scholar at the Woodrow Wilson Center in Washington, DC. She is also the founder of Blue Ink Insights, which brings a social science perspective to companies mapping the environmental and social impacts of their products and services.

Adapted from content posted on hbr.org, November 18, 2022 (product #H07CZC).

about the existence of older workers all. "Today it is socially unacceptable to ignore, ridicule, or stereotype someone based on their gender, race, or sexual orientation," points out Jo Ann Jenkins, the CEO of AARP. "So why is it still acceptable to do this to people based on their age?"[5]

Over the past decades, companies have recognized the economic and social benefits of women, people of color, and LGBT individuals in the workforce. These priority initiatives must be continued—obviously, we're not even close to achieving genuine equality in the corporate world; at the same time, the inclusion of older adults in the business diversity matrix is long overdue. Patricia Milligan, senior partner and global leader for Mercer's Multinational Client Group, observes, "At the most respected multinational companies, the single class not represented from a diversity and inclusion perspective is older workers. LGBT, racial and ethnic diversity, women, people with physical disabilities, veterans—you can find an affinity group in a corporation for everything, except an older worker."

Managing a Multigenerational Workforce

How can companies push past stereotypes and other organizational impediments to tap into a thriving and talented population of older workers? Best practices have been emerging, and some companies are making real progress. Each points to specific changes companies should be considering as they develop their own strategies.

Redefine the workweek

To start, you need to reconsider the out-of-date idea that all employees work Monday through Friday, from nine to five, in the same office. The notion that everyone retires completely by age 65 should also be jettisoned. Companies instead should invest in opportunities for creative mentorship, part-time work, flex-hour schedules, and sabbatical programs geared to the abilities and inclinations of older workers. Programs that offer preretirement and career transition support, coaching, counseling, and encore career pathways can also make employees more engaged and productive. Many older workers say they are ready to exchange high salaries for flexible schedules and phased retirements. Some companies have already embraced nontraditional work programs for employees, creating a new kind of environment for success. The CVS Snowbird program, for example, allows older employees to travel and work seasonally in different CVS pharmacy regions. Home Depot recruits and hires thousands of retired construction workers, making the most of their expertise on the sales floor. The National Institutes of Health, half of whose workforce is over 50, actively recruits at 50-plus job fairs and offers benefits such as flexible schedules, telecommuting, and exercise classes. Steelcase offers workers a phased retirement program with reduced hours. Michelin has rehired retirees to oversee projects, foster community relations, and facilitate employee mentoring. Brooks Brothers consults with older workers on equipment and process design and restructures assignments to offer enhanced flexibility for its aging workforce.

Reimagine the workplace

Your company should also be prepared to adjust workspaces to improve ergonomics and make environments more age-friendly for older employees. No one should be distracted from their tasks by pain that can be prevented or eased, and even small changes can improve health, safety, and productivity. Xerox, for example, has an ergonomic training program aimed at reducing musculoskeletal disorders in its aging workforce. BMW and Nissan have implemented changes to their manufacturing lines to accommodate older workers, ranging from barbershop-style chairs and better-designed tools to "cobot" (collaborative robot) partners that manage complicated tasks and lift heavier objects. The good news is that programs that improve the lives of older workers can be equally valuable for younger counterparts.

Mind the mix

Lastly, you need to consider and monitor the age mixes in your departments and teams. Some pernicious biases can make managing the five-generation workforce difficult. For example, research shows that every generation wants meaningful work—but that each believes everyone else is just in it for the money.[6] Companies should emphasize workers' shared values. "Companies pursuing Millennial-specific employee engagement strategies are wasting time, focus, and money," Bruce Pfau, the former vice chair of human resources at KPMG, argues. "They would be far better served to focus on factors that lead all employees to join, stay, and perform at their best."

By tapping ways that workers of different generations can augment and learn from each other, companies set themselves up for success over the long term. Young workers can benefit from the mentorship of older colleagues, and a promising workforce resource lies in intergenerational collaboration, combining the energy and speed of youth with the wisdom and experience of age.

PNC Financial Group uses multigenerational teams to help the company compete more effectively in the financial markets through a better understanding of the target audience for products. Pharma giant Pfizer has experimented with a "senior intern" program to reap the benefits of multigenerational collaboration. In the tech world, Airbnb recruited former hotel mogul Chip Conley to provide experienced management perspective to his younger colleagues. Pairing younger and older workers in all phases of product and service innovation and design can create opportunity for professional growth. And facilitating intergenerational relationships, mentoring, training, and teaming mitigate isolation and help break down walls.

To begin this process, start talking to your employees of all ages. And get them to talk with each other about their goals, interests, needs, and worries. Young and old workers share similar anxieties and hopes about work—and also have differences that need to be better understood companywide. Look for opportunities for engagement between generations and places where older and younger workers can support one another through skill development and mentorship. After all, if everyone needs and wants to work, we're going to have to learn to work together.

To be clear, all of these changes—from flexible hours to team makeup—will require a recalibration of company processes, some of which are deeply ingrained. Leaders must ask: Do our current health insurance, sick leave, caregiving, and vacation policies accommodate people who work reduced hours? Do our employee performance-measurement systems appropriately recognize and reward the strengths of older workers? Currently, most companies focus on individual achievement as opposed to team success. This may inadvertently punish older employees who offer other types of value—like mentoring, forging deep relationships with clients and colleagues, and resolving conflicts—that are not as easily captured using traditional assessment tools. Here, too, initiatives aimed at older workers can benefit other workers as well. For instance, research suggests that evaluating team performance also tends to boost the careers of employees from low-income backgrounds.[7]

. . .

Initiating a longevity strategy will be a massive culture change for firms—a change that must come from the top. CEOs and senior executives will need to put the issue front and center with HR leaders, product developers, marketing managers, investors, and many other stakeholders who may not have it on their radar screens. This will take guts and persistence: Leaders must bravely say, "We reject the assumption that people become less tech-savvy as they get older" and "We will fight the impulse to put only our youngest employees on new initiatives." To genuinely make headway on this long-range issue, companies will have to make tough, and sometimes unpopular, decisions, especially in a world where short-term results and demands dominate leaders' agendas. But isn't that what great leaders do?

TAKEAWAYS

In many countries worldwide, the population is aging rapidly. Leaders have not yet realized how these societal shifts will affect every aspect of business operations. Organizations need a "longevity strategy" for fostering a vibrant multigenerational workforce. Begin with the following tactics:

- ✓ **Redefine the workweek.** The notion that everyone retires completely by age 65 should be jettisoned. Companies instead should invest in opportunities for creative mentorship, part-time work, flex-hour schedules, and sabbatical programs geared to the abilities and inclinations of older workers.

- ✓ **Reimagine the workplace.** Your company should also be prepared to adjust workspaces to improve ergonomics and make environments more age-friendly for older employees.

✓ **Mind the mix.** By tapping into ways that workers of different generations can augment and learn from each other, companies can set themselves up for success over the long term.

NOTES

1. Kenneth Terrell, "Age Discrimination Common in Workplace, Survey Says," AARP, August 2, 2018, https://www.aarp.org/work /age-discrimination/common-at-work/.

2. Kathleen Pender, "Study Using Fake Resumes Shows Widespread Age Discrimination," *San Francisco Chronicle*, February 27, 2017, https://www.sfchronicle.com/business/networth /article/Study-using-fake-resumes-shows-widespread-age -10963360.php.

3. Gaurav Lahiri and Jeff Schwartz, "The Longevity Dividend: Work in an Era of 100-Year Lives," *Deloitte Insights*, March 28, 2018, https://www2.deloitte.com/us/en/insights/focus/human-capital -trends/2018/advantages-implications-of-aging-workforce.html.

4. John Legere (@johnlegere), "So starting Aug. 9, anyone 55+ can grab . . . ," Twitter, August 7, 2017, https://twitter.com/JohnLegere /status/894531343970729985.

5. Milken Institute, "The Power of Purposeful Aging: Culture Change and the New Democracy," *Report from the 2016 Purposeful Aging Summit* (Washington, DC: Milken Institute Center for Purposeful Aging, 2016), https://milkeninstitute.org/sites/default /files/reports-pdf/PAS-16_2.pdf.

6. Kelly Pledger Weeks, "Every Generation Wants Meaningful Work—but Thinks Other Age Groups Are in It for the Money," hbr .org, July 31, 2017, https://hbr.org/2017/07/every-generation-wants -meaningful-work-but-thinks-other-age-groups-are-in-it-for-the -money.

7. Nicole M. Stephens and Sarah Townsend, "Research: How You Feel About Individualism Is Influenced by Your Social Class," hbr.org, May 22, 2017, https://hbr.org/2017/05/research-how-you -feel-about-individualism-is-influenced-by-your-social-class.

Adapted from "When No One Retires," on hbr.org, November 7, 2018 (product #H04MM9).

3

WHAT REVERSE AGEISM LOOKS LIKE

by Emma Waldman

started my career in New York City, working as an editorial assistant for one of the largest publishing conglomerates in the world. Fresh out of grad school with several years of internship experience in tow, I walked into the 52-story building with my head held high. I was to report directly to the senior vice president, an industry legend. She was poised and intelligent, and I idolized her.

During my second week on the job, I received her email invitation for an in-person meeting. Heart racing, I dashed through the doors of her corner office that overlooked Broadway and West 56th. Expecting to receive my first real assignment, she looked at me and said, "Emma, I just received a package from IKEA. Would you mind assembling my new lamp? Let me know when you're finished."

I would love to dismiss this humiliating—yet humbling—moment as one bad thing that happened a very long time ago. But it still triggers me today: a woman approaching 30 with seven years of job experience under my belt. As one of the youngest people on my team by a decade, I'm often hesitant to assert myself in meetings or ask more seasoned colleagues for help out of fear of seeming naive. In these moments, I find myself back in the corner office, building my first boss's IKEA lamp and trying to figure out her intentions. Was it because I seemed incompetent? Was it because my role included "assistant" in the title?

Or was it what I feared then—and still fear now—that my age makes it hard to take me seriously?

I needed to figure out if this insecurity has grounds in reality. Here's what the research tells me: When you Google "age discrimination at work," you'll find article after article about bias against older employees and laws aimed at addressing this problem. In the United States, the federal government has protections in place to prevent discrimination against workers aged 40 and up. Companies can't, for example, legally assume that someone isn't qualified for a job because they are "too old" to understand how to use a certain technology or implement the latest innovations. That said, it's questionable whether these protections always work. Ageism against older workers still runs rampant in some companies and industries.

At the same time, these protections don't apply to young professionals. This is a problem. A recent study revealed that young adults are often more likely to report experiencing ageism at work than their middle-aged and older counterparts.[1] It's called "reverse ageism."

On top of this, Glassdoor released a 2019 diversity and inclusion survey in the United States, U.K., France, and Germany that found younger employees (52% of ages 18–34) are more likely than older employees (39% of ages 55-plus) to have witnessed or experienced ageism at work.[2]

"Ageism cuts both ways," Professor Dominic Abrams at the University of Kent told me. "It's true that people often apply patronizing stereotypes to older workers, and so they are often assumed to be less employable. But younger people tend to be more exposed to all forms of prejudice and discrimination than older people—racism, sexism, and ageism."

Reverse ageism can show up in many ways. More senior or experienced employees overlooking feedback from younger colleagues on projects. Seasoned employees assuming that younger colleagues can't be trusted with important tasks. Or younger colleagues being the target of stereotypical age assumptions.

When I explore whether these examples fit into my own work experience, I'm brought back to one moment. I was in the office, talking to a fellow 20-something-year-old coworker about an upcoming assignment. We were brainstorming ideas for a new product when a senior employee turned to us and said, "Girls, can you please take your chatter elsewhere? It's very distracting."

My peer and I exchanged a glance—confused, and a little bit shocked. While our colleague may have thought he was just asking for quiet, there were assumptions embedded in his comment:

Assumption 1: That we were "girls," not two grown women.

Assumption 2: Our discussion was "chatter," as if we weren't working on anything of importance.

So no, not all of it was in my head.

I understand how it might be easy for people to mistrust those who have less workplace experience than themselves, but this mistrust ultimately works against all of us and can lead to biased assumptions. When older workers doubt the competency of those younger than them, they fail us. They are not helping the next generations develop transferable skills. They're building barriers of mistrust.

Will It Get Better?

Discrimination varies from person to person, and for this reason, organizations often struggle to tackle these biases on a wider scale. You can't force someone to think a certain way, but you can help them to better understand your position and perspective.

Here are a few ideas I've started to put into practice. They may help you if you're experiencing reverse ageism. And if you manage others, make sure that all of your employees—regardless of age—understand what reverse ageism looks like and how they can combat it.

Start or join a working group for young professionals

Keeping quiet about discrimination at work can be both mentally and emotionally draining—and can bleed into your life outside of the office over time. It's important to create a safe space to talk to people you trust about what you're going through. If your company doesn't already have a working group for young professionals, consider starting one yourself. This might take the form of a designated Slack channel in which you can talk openly and share experiences online. Or it might be a monthly Zoom call with a proposed agenda and discussion points. Either way, it will give people like yourself a place to talk about workplace concerns, find allies, and exchange ideas about how to remedy them.

Talk to your manager

Make your manager aware of the situation. They may have no idea what you're going through. During your next check-in, share your experiences and concerns. They might redirect you to an HR specialist who is trained in handling issues of discrimination at work, or help you devise a plan for confronting the perpetrator. If anything, your manager will know to keep their eyes peeled for future instances of ageism. Raising the issue is the first step towards combating it for good.

Alternatively, your manager might understand workplace discrimination all too well and be able to serve as a role model and mentor in the future. One of my workplace mentors is a woman who has just as much professional experience as her male counterparts (if not more).

Because we've both fallen victim to other workplace biases (in terms of gender discrimination) in the past, she was sympathetic toward my situation. She knew what it was like to feel undervalued because of something that's out of your control and offered me some actionable suggestions for overcoming these biases in the future.

Have an open discussion with the culprit

There's nothing wrong with respectfully approaching the coworker who is demonstrating discrimination against you to have an open dialogue. Sending an email that begins with, "The comment that you made during Tuesday's meeting made me feel uncomfortable. When you bring my age into a conversation, it sounds like you're assuming that I'm not qualified to do my job," is a great place to start. This could evolve into a larger conversation about ageism and how to overcome biases that might be clouding their judgment. If you feel comfortable, you could suggest working on a project together to build trust and demonstrate your expertise. You might even end up learning more about where this person's bias is coming from.

You might find, for example, that the culprit's behavior stems from an insecurity about their own performance and has nothing to do with you personally (though this is still not an excuse for their behavior).

Never forget the value you add

When you're put down by someone at work, it can be easy to forget your value. But I can reassure you: You offer a special skill set and a unique perspective, which is why you were hired. Figure out what your "specialty" is—whether it's social media proficiency, communication skills, expertise with video or audio platforms, etc.—and use it to your advantage. When the opportunity presents itself, remind your coworkers of what you bring to the table. You have insights and experiences that others do not.

Most importantly, let these experiences inform your growth as you advance in your career. Don't let the fear that you'll never be taken seriously stay with you until you're old enough to be considered "seasoned." Set an example by trusting and asserting that young professionals know what they're doing, and strive to become the kind of employee you'd want to work with, years down the line, when a young colleague approaches you for help.

TAKEAWAYS

Young adults are more likely to report experiencing ageism at work than their older counterparts—but they are not protected by law from age discrimination. Reverse age discrimination may manifest as senior or more experienced employees overlooking feedback from younger colleagues, assuming they can't be trusted, or targeting them with stereotypical assumptions. Younger workers—as well as managers and allies—should understand and employ the following tactics to deal with reverse ageism.

✓ **Start or join a working group for young professionals.** It will provide a space to talk about workplace concerns, find allies, and exchange ideas about how to remedy problems.

✓ **Talk to your manager.** They may have no idea what you're going through and can give you tools to help you navigate it.

✓ **Have an open discussion with the culprit.** There's nothing wrong with respectfully approaching the coworker who is demonstrating discrimination.

✓ **Never forget the value you add.** You bring a special skill set to the office, which is why you were hired.

NOTES

1. Christopher Bratt, Dominic Abrams, and Hannah J. Swift, "Supporting the Old but Neglecting the Young? The Two Faces of Ageism," *Developmental Psychology* 56 (May 2020): 1029–1039.

2. Glassdoor, "Diversity and Inclusion Study 2019," https://about -content.glassdoor.com/app/uploads/sites/2/2019/10/Glassdoor -Diversity-Survey-Supplement-1.pdf.

Adapted from "Am I Old Enough to Be Taken Seriously?" on Ascend, hbr.org, November 25, 2020.

4

HELPING GEN Z EMPLOYEES FIND THEIR PLACE AT WORK

by Jenny Fernandez, Julie Lee, and Kathryn Landis

Gen Z, born approximately between 1995 and 2010, is the most racially and ethnically diverse generation in U.S. history. This generation has also been influenced by, and is influential in, the macro social movements and systemic issues that have shaped who they are and what they stand for in the workplace and society. They've played crucial roles in movements fighting racism and discrimination, sexual harassment, gun violence, and worsening climate change, as growing income disparity makes the possibility of social mobility more unrealistic than ever.

All of this was exacerbated by Covid-19. The pandemic devastated the U.S. economy and stopped the longest streak of growth in decades. As Gen Z entered the workforce, many were quickly furloughed or fired. All these factors in combination fueled Gen Z's disillusionment with the establishment and capitalism. Thus, this group garnered a reputation for mistrust of the status quo, disconnection, and impatience, and for demanding immediate action around issues it cares about.

Despite their turbulent transition to adulthood, Gen Z is already shaping and influencing society and the workplace in numerous ways. The results of the 2022 U.S. midterm elections revealed Gen Z's collective power as its political choices swayed election results. In addition, Gen Z employees are bringing their values and priorities to work, particularly their desire for transparency around recognition and rewards, and have started to make a significant impact. However, research shows that Gen Z may be struggling with engagement at work. According to a 2022 Gallup Poll, 54% of Gen Z employees, slightly higher than any other generation, are ambivalent or not engaged at work.[1]

As such, it is essential for managers to support their Gen Z employees and earn their full engagement. Here are seven strategies you can leverage to create a team dynamic of collaboration, commitment, and sustained motivation.

Increase Information Sharing to Alleviate Fears of Uncertainty

Gen Z is the first fully digital native generation, having grown up with extensive access to information in real time. Having experienced economic uncertainty driven by a global health pandemic, Gen Z had to contend with what the U.S. Surgeon General Dr. Vivek Murthy is calling a youth mental health crisis. The result is a working cohort that is experiencing a lack of control and uncertainty about the future and is "reporting higher rates of anxiety, depression, and distress than any other age group."[2]

Thus, to build trust and a stronger connection with this generation, you must prioritize transparency and shift your managing and communication style from a "need to know" policy to an "open access" one. This is true even if the news or information you are holding back is meant to "protect" employees from stress or fear, such as when business performance is not meeting targets, supply chain issues are on the rise, or you may need to cut their budget. Access to information will alleviate Gen Z's anxieties and allow them to process and feel in control.

To think about how you can improve, start reflecting on the following questions and discuss them with your team:

- Do I currently have a two-way dialogue with team members across multiple communication mediums? Confirm with your team which communication methods they prefer and align on a realistic frequency of consistent interaction.

- Have I made room to share and discuss the team's strategy and impact on the organization? Does the team know how their role impacts the strategy? Discuss with your team what assumptions need to be true for them to meet their goals. Do they feel empowered to succeed?

- Do I leverage our team meetings to discuss results, performance, and future outlook, given the impact of new information? Discuss openly and honestly your outlook of the future and what is impacting the business. Ask your team if they feel empowered and supported to achieve their goals.

- Do I regularly ask the team for feedback about where we need more transparency or clarity (e.g., clear roles and responsibilities, expectations, etc.)? Make the necessary adjustments and acknowledgments to make team members feel seen and heard.

Show Them Paths to Career Progression to Incentivize Them

Gen Z is pragmatic and concerned with job security and advancement. According to the Pew Research Center, "half of the oldest Gen Zers (ages 18 to 23) reported that they or someone in their household had lost a job or taken a cut in pay because of the [Covid-19] outbreak."[3] Thus, understanding performance metrics, what "good" looks like, and how to overdeliver is key. These employees want to know what is expected of them to advance and how they can be in control of their future. Be sure to explain to them what it means to succeed as an individual contributor and future leader. If your company has a matrixed organization, for example, explain how relationship building, influencing, and team collaboration impact overall performance, as success is not measured simply in results but also in how the work is done and the impact on others.

Pay equity is also a priority for Gen Z. Conduct group discussions about salaries so this generation sees the organization's commitment to it. For example, with 1.1 billion views and nearly 21 million likes, TikTok account Salary Transparent Street features people from different U.S. cities sharing their profession and salary. As Gen Zers

Dear CEOs: A Gen Zer's Open Letter to His Future Employers

by Khalil Greene

Kahlil Greene, a senior at Yale who served as the first Black student body president, takes us inside the conversations among Gen Zers deciding where to work. He offers unvarnished advice for today's corporate leaders to help them build a bridge between generational mindsets and understand what tomorrow's leaders need to succeed.

We know you want to create a diverse, inclusive, and great place to work for current and future generations. However, you are often not given the unvarnished feedback on why it is so difficult to make this happen. For your sake, and for ours, let me clue you into our decision process and share what often goes unsaid.

If you're still making the business case for diversity, your company isn't the place for us

As a freshman, I attended an investment banking event for underrepresented minorities where a recruiter told us about the efforts of the company's diversity recruiting team. The team struggled to get adequate buy-in and investment to build a more diverse and inclusive workplace. What finally broke the inertia was a robust business case that proved that diversity was good for profits. It told me that they may not value ideas I bring to the workplace unless there was a direct link to revenue growth. I stopped considering working there after that session. As one of my peers recounted, "If you care about your people, you care about what your people care about."

We want companies to take a stand

Gen Zers grew up in the era of social movements like #Black-LivesMatter and #MeToo. For most of our lives, we've been immersed in fast-paced political discussions on social media. Regardless of our political leanings, we've always known the importance of taking a stand. For us, it's more about our values and expectations of social justice than politics.

(continued)

Dear CEOs: A Gen Zer's Open Letter to His Future Employers (*continued*)

We are works in progress

We are America's most diverse generation, but many of us are still the "firsts" in our families and communities. We're not fluent in the language and social conventions of corporate America. We need to learn a new vocabulary to belong.

We want to be ourselves

As digital natives, we can be assets to the companies where we work. We're adept at a range of technology tools and services—whether it's Facebook marketing or Google ads or gamification.

So, when we're presented with a multi-page compliance manual that severely limits—or worse, forbids—our use of social media, we're inclined to search for an environment that can provide similar work and pay while allowing us to bring our whole selves (even our social media selves) to work.

We want to make an impact

Gen Zers are highly motivated to support social progress in our nation. For many of us, this is no longer a "nice-to-have." We want a workplace where we can support non-profit and social impact organizations and take on passion projects that do well for society.

Gen Zers will soon take over Corporate America. We are coming in with high standards for ourselves; we want to contribute to the companies we join and the societies of which we are a part. My hope is that this "straight talk" is a step toward building a bridge between generations and mindsets, so we can collectively create an inclusive and prosperous future.

Kahlil Greene is a Gen Z workplace inclusion expert. He was the first-ever fellow at ghSMART & Co. He graduated in 2022 from Yale University, where he served as its first Black student body president. His mission is to bridge the gap between Gen Z and the corporate world with the diversity, equity, and inclusion standards of a new generation.

Adapted from content posted on hbr.org, June 29, 2021 (product #H06FWZ).

are sharing the salary information openly with one another, they expect their employers to share the information more openly and affirm organizational commitment to pay equity. Having conversations about salary and career progression in the open will go a long way with Gen Z.

Explain How Their Individual Contributions Matter

McKinsey research confirms Gen Z is a purpose-driven generation.[4] Their desire to know how their individual contributions and role in the team help support the organization's mission differentiates them. They make career choices and purchasing choices driven by the impact these make in the world. Thus, managers should consider setting up sessions to speak about the team's vision and impact on the organization. We all need to understand our roles and responsibilities to do our jobs, but Gen Z needs to understand how and why their role matters. Here are some steps you can take to facilitate these discussions:

- Invite each team member to briefly share their unique skills, capabilities, and growth areas with the rest of the team. Also, ask each team member individually for their suggestions and ideas on how to best contribute and obtain opportunities for development.

- Create a dialogue about how each person uniquely contributes to the team and its overall impact. This exercise will be beneficial to Gen Z to visualize how their efforts play a role in the greater good.

Moreover, take time to explain how the broader organizational goals have a positive impact on the world. This will help overcome the perception that business prioritizes their own agendas over the good of society, with no ambition beyond making money.

Give Them Room for Autonomy to Keep Them Motivated

Having grown up with unfettered access to information, Gen Z seeks to make informed decisions on their own. They need room for experimentation to prove themselves. Thus, in order to keep them motivated, flex your management style and give them greater room and autonomy to explore and figure out improvements in work processes. They might surprise you with a better outcome.

Create opportunities for these workers to lean in on their strengths such as leveraging technology, social media, and their desire for connection. It's a new way to enroll them in your vision while driving engagement.

Provide Specific, Constructive Feedback to Demonstrate That You Are Invested in Their Success

Annual feedback is a great recap of what happens in the year but often does not create an opportunity to learn, optimize, and pivot to make an impact on the outcome in real time. Look to provide continuous, clear feedback with real-life examples of what is working or not working, and action steps that increase your Gen Z team's self-awareness. Take this as a coaching opportunity and provide them with prompt questions that allow them to reflect and explore different outcomes.

Here are three questions for your Gen Z direct reports:

- What does success look like in a given situation?

- What are you learning from this particular work-stream or project?

- What has been challenging for you on the team and what suggestions do you have for improving?

Also, support them by elevating their situational awareness. For many, this will be the first time working in person, getting direct constructive feedback, and building professional relationships. They might not realize the impact of their actions on the broader team. Consider having a group discussion or training on how to build resilience and emotional intelligence to succeed in the workplace and how to approach feedback as a lifelong self-improvement journey.

Harness Community and Connection to Engage and Empower Them

NYU Stern Professor, social psychologist, and author Johnathan Haidt said: "The more connected a generation is, the more lonely it is." While this is the most connected generation with technology, social media, and smartphones, Gen Z is also among the most isolated. The Cigna U.S. Loneliness Index found that "[a]mong workers aged 18–22 . . . 73% report sometimes or always feeling alone."[5] Most Gen Z employees know only remote or hybrid ways of life. Thus, they haven't had as many opportunities to forge deep professional relationships that are often created in person over a period of time.

As a manager, you may consider giving them location work autonomy to choose their desired hybrid/remote working structure. Autonomy of choice has been proven to increase employee engagement. However, you must also create opportunities for in-person interactions that will create connections and camaraderie such as team-building activities, project kickoffs, team celebrations, and state-of-the-business discussions. Creating shared team experiences like these will help develop stronger bonds. And while in-person interactions are ideal for team building, intentional remote activities will also help. Two examples include scheduling a virtual "coffee chat" during business hours when team members can drop in and connect with colleagues informally or making a plan to recognize a contribution of one member during a team meeting.

You may also consider supporting this generation by creating a mentoring program with Millennial and Gen X employees to bridge across generations and to boost meaningful collaboration across age cohorts. In addition, create a peer or buddy program where you pair Gen Z team members together so that they always have someone to contact for support. This is mutually beneficial, as Gallup research reports that having a best friend at work is key to employee engagement and job success.[6] It is "strongly linked to business outcomes, including profitability, safety, inventory control, and retention."

Prioritize Wellness and Mental Health to Show You Care

Mental health struggles are a crucial factor impacting Gen Z employees. Many experience anxiety and depression, which affects their work performance. In fact, Gen Z's top wish for their leadership is that they care about well-being and mental health.[7] As a leader, it is your shared responsibility not just to elevate the team's performance but also to support their well-being to perform at their best. Thus, organizations and leaders must create a culture, practices, and resources that support Gen Z's mental wellness.

To start, ask your team members how they are doing. Lead by example and share your emotional state, worries, and coping mechanisms. Empathy goes a long way to create a shared connection and open up avenues of communication and deeper conversation. Then, work to create a team culture that allows for vulnerability and open communication and makes time for mental recovery. Addressing what impacts the team will improve their overall effectiveness and allow you to manage timelines and priorities around mental wellness just as you would for physical illness.

Next, you can implement benefits and practices that help the mental health of Gen Z. For instance, LinkedIn started offering its employees additional time off to address burnout among their workforce. Similarly, there are a number of technology companies and startups that are offering, or even in some cases mandating, mental health days off for their workforce.

Another opportunity is to offer and support mental health–related employee resource groups (ERGs). When supporting Gen Z employees from diverse backgrounds, it is critical to offer culturally responsive resources as some cohorts, such as Black and Hispanic members of Gen Z, tend to underutilize these resources. To empower yourself to have these rich conversations, ask your organization to provide you with training opportunities to learn about mental health–related benefits and policies or communication tools with which you can effectively discuss mental health issues.

. . .

The global pandemic and the macro social movements that have shaped Gen Z have changed the rules of the game in the workplace. More than any other generation, this cohort is looking to those in positions of authority to prove themselves with transparency and follow-through. You can support them in their professional development by demonstrating your investment in their success, flexing your management style, and communicating inclusively.

Research shows that Gen Z is struggling with engagement at work. According to Gallup, a higher proportion of Gen Z employees are ambivalent or not engaged at work than any other generation. It is essential for managers to support their Gen Z employees and earn their full engagement.

- ✓ Increase information sharing to alleviate fears of uncertainty

- ✓ Show them paths to career progression to incentivize them

- ✓ Explain how their individual contributions matter

- ✓ Give them room for autonomy to keep them motivated

✓ Provide specific, constructive feedback to demonstrate investment in their success

✓ Harness community and connection to engage and empower them

✓ Prioritize their wellness and mental health

NOTES

1. Ryan Pendell and Sara Vander Helm, "Generation Disconnected: Data on Gen Z in the Workplace," Gallup Workplace, November 11, 2022, https://www.gallup.com/workplace/404693 /generation-disconnected-data-gen-workplace.aspx.

2. Erica Coe et al., "Addressing the Unprecedented Behavioral Health Challenges Facing Generation Z," McKinsey & Company, January 14, 2022, https://www.mckinsey.com/industries /healthcare/our-insights/addressing-the-unprecedented -behavioral-health-challenges-facing-generation-z.

3. Kim Parker and Ruth Igielnik, "On the Cusp of Adulthood and Facing an Uncertain Future: What We Know about Gen Z So Far," Pew Research Center, May 14, 2020, https://www.pewresearch.org /social-trends/2020/05/14/on-the-cusp-of-adulthood-and-facing -an-uncertain-future-what-we-know-about-gen-z-so-far-2/.

4. Tracy Francis and Fernanda Hoeful, "'True Gen': Generation Z and Its Implications for Companies," McKinsey & Company, November 12, 2018, https://www.mckinsey.com/industries/consumer -packaged-goods/our-insights/true-gen-generation-z-and-its -implications-for-companies.

5. Bertha Coombs, "Loneliness Is on the Rise and Younger Workers and Social Media Users Feel It Most, Cigna Survey Finds," CNBC, January 23, 2020, https://www.cnbc.com/2020/01/23/loneliness-is-rising-younger-workers-and-social-media-users-feel-it-most.html.

6. Alok Patel and Stephanie Plowman, "The Increasing Importance of a Best Friend at Work," Gallup Workplace, August 17, 2022, https://www.gallup.com/workplace/397058/increasing-importance-best-friend-work.aspx.

7. Ed O'Boyle, "4 Things Gen Z and Millennials Expect from Their Workplace," Gallup Workplace, March 30, 2021, https://www.gallup.com/workplace/336275/things-gen-millennials-expect-workplace.aspx.

Adapted from content posted on hbr.org, January 18, 2023 (product #H07FI3).

CARING FOR YOUR COMPANY'S CAREGIVERS

by Sarita Gupta and Ai-jen Poo

A few years ago, Joy Johnston flew across the country to help care for her father, who had Alzheimer's. After she quickly used up the significant amount of paid time off she had accrued at her job, she applied for federal Family and Medical Leave Act (FMLA) benefits, but this proved difficult—her father regularly moved facilities, and the FMLA approval process requires a complicated array of hospital verification documents.

After her father died, Joy switched jobs. Six months later, her mother was diagnosed with colon cancer. Joy had accrued no paid time off and was not yet eligible to apply for FMLA benefits, and her employer refused to let her work remotely when her mother had surgery. Put in this difficult situation, Joy quit. She was able to scrape together a handful of remote jobs, but earned only a quarter of what she had been making before. She also lacked employer-sponsored health insurance and couldn't afford to contribute to a retirement account.

Messy and difficult sagas like Joy's are only becoming more common. By 2050, the U.S. population of older adults will have nearly doubled, to 83.7 million people.[1] Pew estimates that nearly 40% of adults in the United States are unpaid caregivers, and the AARP notes that six in 10 family caregivers are also in the labor force.[2]

Thriving into our eighties, nineties, and even hundreds will be impossible without help, and caregiving usually falls on family members, many of whom are faced with having to give up careers and income to help an ailing parent. This problem disproportionately affects women, who overwhelmingly outnumber men in caregiving roles. They also tend to take on more difficult care tasks than men, such as bathing, toileting, and dressing, while men are more likely to assist with less burdensome tasks, such as finances and arrangement of care.[3]

Almost all of this work is unpaid—and the financial penalties associated with it are striking. What's more, caregiving also interrupts careers: In a study of prime-age workers not in the workforce, 36% of unemployed women had left work as a result of caregiving, compared to only 3% of men.[4]

This situation will surely continue; along with parenting, balancing work and caring for older family members will become a central struggle for Americans over the next several decades. Many of these people are your employees—or will be. Along with home care workers, they're part of an invisible and struggling economy. In order to truly address the needs of an older America, we need to change the way we approach caregiving itself—and businesses have a crucial role to play.

What Companies Are—and Aren't—Doing

Until now, the burdens of this new world have fallen on workers, not their employers. Fully 68% of working family caregivers report making adjustments at work such as arriving late or leaving early, taking time off, changing jobs, turning down a promotion, or cutting back on hours. Workers in the "sandwich generation"—so called because they have to care for both children and parents—are likely to be hit the hardest; according to Gallup work-force data reported in *Fast Company*, about one-third of American managers are part of Generation X. A full 11% of them care for an elderly or disabled person, while 64% have children living at home. Millennials are now being affected as well, making up about 25% of the nation's family caregivers; like members of Generation X, many of their parents are aging Baby Boomers.[5] Older workers are affected, too: 19% report retiring early, not because they're ready to leave the workforce, but because they need to care for a spouse or other family member.

Companies are failing to meet the needs of some of their most experienced and talented workers across the generations. What's more, they risk losing these workers to companies that are on the cutting edge of responding and adapting to caregiving responsibilities brought on by an aging nation.

One company that is often cited as progressive in this area is L.L. Bean. Headquartered in Freeport, Maine, L.L. Bean's employees range in age from 16 to 91, with an average age of 49. "Our approach is to be an employer with 'ageless appeal,'" wrote the firm's director of human resources, Wendy Estabrook, in a 2015 article in *Maine Policy Review*.[6] Flexibility in the workplace at L.L. Bean takes many different forms. In addition to its full-time employees, L.L. Bean has employees at three part-time levels (on call, seasonal, and active retiree) and offers the option of working remotely. When it comes to leave, the company augments FMLA with its own leave policy that allows employees to take up to six months in a 12-month period away from work, unpaid, to care for themselves or a loved one. On top of this, the company offers counseling on the myriad issues that arise around care, whether related to locating resources, dealing with financial or legal issues, or coping with grief.

"We have actually found that typically what is good for the 25-year-old is also good for the 55-year-old employee although that may be for different reasons," Estabrook wrote. In other words, the policies that can help a 45-year-old employee work remotely while caring for her aging mother or allow a 30-year-old dad to take leave to spend time with his new baby will also help a 65-year-old who wants to stay in the workforce. Across the age and work spectrums, flexibility makes a world of difference.

But flexible workplaces don't just emerge organically; they require years of development and a serious commitment to shifting workplace culture. A culture that benefits both the parents of children and the children of parents has to be supported by top executives in the workplace and must be incorporated into the hiring process of every employee, notes Drew Holzapfel, a partner at the High Lantern Group consultancy and a member of ReACT, a coalition of companies that advocates for caregivers.

Holzapfel points to Emory University, which has established a culture of care throughout the institution, facilitated through its WorkLife Resource Center. The process began in 2010, when a campuswide needs assessment found that 15% of the respondents were caring for an older, ill, or disabled family member and more than half were concerned about balancing the responsibilities of work and care in the next one to three years. The university convened an adult-care working group, including human resources professionals, experts on aging, social workers, and elder law attorneys, to address the needs of employees. The group came up with a set of recommendations: expanding the university's family medical and sick leave policies, developing and promoting an employer-sponsored adult-care program, providing on-call emergency backup home care, increasing awareness of available resources, promoting the cultural inclusion of care issues through counseling and workshops, and hiring a dedicated work-life adviser to oversee the program and provide one-on-one coaching and support for employees.

These policies were implemented five years ago. "We have surveyed our workforce twice in recent years and see that flexibility is increasing all across our campus.

Over half of our workforce reports working flexibly," said Audrey Adelson, a consultant at Emory's WorkLife Resource Center. "The shift to flexible work has not been easy and is a cultural change that takes time and effort, but it has been worth it."

Providing a range of care support to your employees may sound expensive, but in the long term, it can improve a company's bottom line. A joint report by AARP and ReACT found that supportive caregiving policies have a high return on investment.[7]

Moreover, family-friendly policies also help recruit new talent. In one survey of college students, the availability of flextime, elder care benefits, and paid family leave were shown to influence the job choices of up to 33% of job seekers.[8] Overall, flexible work hours lead to 50% less absenteeism, 30% increased employee retention, and 20% better recruitment.[9] Research also shows that companies with such policies have some of the highest net promoter scores—that is, they are most likely to be recommended by their employees as great places to work.[10]

Larger companies are starting to catch on: Starbucks recently announced that it would offer heavily subsidized backup care to both full-time and part-time employees for 10 days per year. Even Silicon Valley, with its still relatively young workforce, has made early advances in accommodating caregiving needs. Many companies offer generous paid leave for new parents. These examples show that the most pioneering companies are not waiting for new regulations or more support from the government but are acting on their own. They are taking a broader, much more flexible approach to caregiving that reflects the needs of an aging society.

Steps Your Organization Can Take Now

Adapting your company's caregiving culture isn't always easy. But here are two places to start.

First, offer flexible benefits (rather than simply maternity or childcare leave). This normalizes taking leave for *anyone*. Care isn't just something that young women do for their children; a middle-aged man or an older employee may equally need to take time off. Framing the benefit as care leave and offering it as a paid benefit takes away the stigma around both maternity leave and elder care and reduces the stereotype that women should be primary caregivers. Companies may need to encourage their male employees to take parental leave—research has shown that when a few men take leave, other men follow suit.[11] Humanyze, a people analytics company, actually *requires* new fathers to take parental leave.

Second, reduce the stigma attached to care needs and responsibilities. We have been culturally conditioned to refrain from talking about care needs or caregiving responsibilities when we are at work, especially with our bosses. Companies can begin to change this in subtle and explicit ways.

One approach is to encourage employees to self-identify as caregivers—particularly those who typically don't reveal themselves to be in caregiving roles, such as men, young people, and senior managers. This can start during the training process for new employees. Human resources departments can bring in experts to talk about caregiving, encouraging employees to feel more open in sharing their experiences and how caregiving impacts their work. Companies also can offer access to therapy and counseling as part of employees' health benefits.

Just as corporate gyms, yoga studios, and lactation rooms are becoming part of the design of many corporate campuses, companies should consider designing workspaces using photos, symbols, and artifacts that emphasize our shared caregiving roles and need for care. For example, managers can have photos of older parents, children, or pets on their desk as a way of affirming these roles. Companies could also host days on which employees can bring grandparents, parents, or children to work, or extend invitations to family members for company events.

One of us (Sarita) took a full 12 weeks of parental leave when she had her daughter, Suraiya. She made a point of disconnecting from work as a way of encouraging other new parents to do the same. Given her own caregiving responsibilities, she frequently uses our policies on remote work, and she takes paid sick days and leave when Suraiya or her parents have medical needs. She has also been mindful of creating a family-friendly office culture, bringing her daughter to the office and her parents to major events. She has pictures of her family on her desk and acknowledges team members' pictures when they have them displayed, too.

All of these steps can help normalize and affirm care needs and responsibilities in the workplace. This is uncharted territory for most organizations, however, so these shifts should be approached as a series of experiments or small steps before they are codified as best practices.

Of course, companies can't solve our caregiving problem entirely. We also need broader public-sector solutions that acknowledge the evolving state of the caregiving workforce and provide working family caregivers with supports that address their growing and changing needs. Ultimately, we need to recognize that care work is vital to our society. Businesses can and should play a huge role in making this cultural shift, driven in no small part by company leaders. In valuing your employees' commitment to the people they love the most, you're showing that you value them, too.

A growing portion of the workforce consists of unpaid caregivers of aging parents, young children, and other family members. Many of these workers are faced with having to give up careers to care for others, and this problem disproportionately affects women. Companies that fail to help these caregivers are neglecting to meet the needs of some of their most experienced and talented workers across generations—and risk losing them to companies with better policies.

✓ Start by offering flexible benefits—family leave rather than simply maternity or childcare leave. This normalizes taking leave for *anyone*.

✓ Work to reduce the stigma attached to care needs and responsibilities. We have been culturally conditioned to refrain from talking about caregiving responsibilities at work. Companies can begin to change this in subtle and explicit ways.

✓ Companies can't solve the caregiving problem entirely. We also need broader public-sector solutions for working family caregivers with resources that address their growing and changing needs.

NOTES

1. U.S. Census Bureau, "Fueled by Aging Baby Boomers, Nation's Older Population to Nearly Double Over the Next 20 Years," press release no. CB14084, May 6, 2014, https://www.census.gov /newsroom/archives/2014-pr/cb14-84.html.

2. Drew DeSilver, "As Population Ages, More Americans Becoming Caregivers," Pew Research Center, July 18, 2013, https://www .pewresearch.org/fact-tank/2013/07/18/as-population-ages-more -americans-becoming-caregivers/; Lynn Friss Feinberg, "The Dual Pressures of Family Caregiving and Employment," AARP, May 2016, https://www.aarp.org/content/dam/aarp/ppi/2016-03 /The-Dual-Pressures-off-Family-Caregiving-and-Employment.pdf.

3. Caregiver Statistics Demographics, Family Caregiver Alliance, n.d., https://www.caregiver.org/resource/caregiver-statistics -demographics/.

4. Whitmore Schazenback et al., "Who Is Out of the Labor Force?" The Hamilton Project, August 17, 2017, http://www .hamiltonproject.org/papers/who_is_out_of_the_labor_force.

5. Lydia Dishman, "The Overlooked Benefit Gen X Workers Need," *Fast Company*, May 7, 2018, https://www.fastcompany.com /40568411/the-overlooked-benefit-gen-x-workers-need.

6. Wendy Eastabrook, "Older Workers at L.L. Bean," *Maine Policy Review* 24, no. 2 (2015): 67–68.

7. Sarah Walker, "Employer's Guide to Supporting Employees with Caregiving Responsibilities," Respect Care Givers, May 2, 2022, https://respectcaregivers.org/employers-guide-supporting -employees-caregiving-responsibilities/.

8. Lori Foster Thompson and Kimberly R. Aspinwall, "The Recruitment Value of Work/Life Benefits," *Personnel Review* 38, no. 2 (2009): 195–210.

9. Walker, "Employer's Guide."

10. Emal Hakikat, "How Flexible Working Increases Net Promoter Scores," *Insider HR*, March 10, 2016, https://www.insidehr .com.au/how-flexible-working-increases-net-promoter-scores/.

11. Gretchen Gavett, "Brave Men Take Paternity Leave," hbr.org, July 7, 2014, https://hbr.org/2014/07/brave-men-take-paternity -leave.

Adapted from content posted on hbr.org, November 13, 2018 (product #H04MMD).

6

IT'S TIME TO START TALKING ABOUT MENOPAUSE AT WORK

by Jeneva Patterson

Menopause is rarely a topic of open discussion in the workplace—despite the fact that roughly half of the world's population experiences or will experience this biological transition, which marks the end of a woman's menstrual cycle and fertility. According to the Society for Endocrinology, a startling one in four women will experience serious menopause symptoms.

Menopause often intersects with a critical career stage. It usually occurs between ages 45 and 55—which is also the age bracket during which women are most likely to move into top leadership positions (technically 53.46 years old for a CEO). Since menopause generally lasts between seven and 14 years, millions of postmenopausal women are coming into management and top leadership roles while experiencing mild to severe symptoms such as depression, anxiety, sleep deprivation, and cognitive impairment, to name a few. A recent Korn Ferry analysis finds that women hold only around 25% of C-suite positions.[1] If we want to continue to move the needle on the number of women in leadership roles and maintain their valuable contributions to a company's bottom line, I believe we need to be more open about what menopause is and how it affects both individuals and organizations.

Some researchers suggest that workplace ageism also plays a part in the exclusion of menopausal symptoms from corporate health policies. Companies can be wary of hiring and/or accommodating older employees' health needs. "We find [aging women] kind of disposable or marginal—so it doesn't surprise me that something that impacts older women in particular would be not only a discomfort but a nonconcern," explained Chris Bobel, an associate professor of gender studies at UMass Boston.

Like a lot of women, I instinctually disguised my symptoms when menopause began for me. It was a sharp difference from when I was pregnant—during that time, I didn't think twice about confessing forgetfulness and fatigue. Men and women laughed knowingly and supportively at my anecdotes. But menopause was different. I wouldn't reveal the cause, despite getting lost (even with a GPS), arriving late to important meetings, double- and triple-booking calendar time slots, missing flights, and not even being able to recall what someone had said to me just a few minutes earlier.

When my symptoms began, I was convinced that, at age 48, I had early-onset Alzheimer's disease. Too afraid to discuss my difficulties with anyone at work, I made excuses for my forgetfulness and backed off from a career-enhancing role. How could I take on a bigger challenge when I kept forgetting key details about my projects? When my physician diagnosed menopause, it was a relief and a surprise.

Other women I've spoken to about this experience have echoed how difficult it can be to manage menopause symptoms and work. "Moderating that high-profile panel, in front of 200 industry experts, should have been a career highlight. It was a disaster," grumbled Sandala (not her real name), a 46-year-old biotech vice president.

"Those years of confusion, self-doubt, and severe anxiety practically killed my entire career," Enia (also disguised), a 51-year-old tech executive, told me.

In Enia's case, her symptoms became so severe that two years of damaging 360-degree feedback and deteriorating results led to her dismissal. Today, she works as a diversity-and-inclusion consultant for organizations that are accommodating a broader range of women's health issues. With a twist of irony, her former employer now engages Enia as a consultant. She's happier and healthier than ever.

In retrospect, Enia wishes she'd been more courageous and spoken up about her need for support. Any taboo topic loses power when someone with authority addresses it openly. We are learning to discuss race, gender, and generational differences more openly at work, and we need to put menopause on the agenda.

What can employers do? Based on my experiences, it starts with talking. If you are a leader going through menopause, try to normalize your challenges so that other women can feel empowered to speak in the future. Just saying something like, "I'm going through menopause, and I keep forgetting things!" shows others this is something that is OK to talk about. Dialogue costs nothing but reaps big rewards.

It also takes education. There's a lot of mystery and misinformation about this life stage, and just gathering some basic facts from trusted medical sources is a good start.

Managers can work to bring this issue into the daylight by focusing on its connection to employee well-being—after all, menopause is one of the many health issues that can contribute to stress and burnout. Talk with the women and men on your team about how you might approach accommodation strategies like flexible work schedules, offering options to work from home, or providing company information sessions. Through active leadership support, an organization can begin to realize benefits in productivity, work culture, and the bottom line when menopausal transition is addressed as a specific, work-related concern.

When I went through this, my initial fear of embarrassment stopped me from getting the support I needed. Finally, when it was too hard to continue pretending that nothing was amiss, I said in a 12-person meeting: "I'll have to excuse myself for a few minutes. I'm having a hot flash and need a break." In that moment, I felt powerful, self-assured, and relieved. Everyone nodded like it was no big deal. After the meeting two colleagues approached me to share their own experiences. That encouraged me to speak about my symptoms more often, and I hope my experience inspires others to do the same.

TAKEAWAYS

Millions of postmenopausal women are coming into management and executive roles while experiencing mild to severe symptoms such as depression, anxiety, sleep deprivation, and cognitive impairment. Yet menopause is rarely a topic of open discussion in the workplace. If we want to continue to move the needle on the number of women in leadership roles and maintain their valuable contributions, we need to understand and normalize the effect of menopause in the workplace.

✓ Taboo topics lose power when someone with authority addresses them openly. Managers can work to bring this issue into the daylight by focusing on its connection to employee well-being—after all, menopause is one of the many health issues that can contribute to stress and burnout.

✓ If you are a leader going through menopause, try to normalize your challenges and speak about them. This will empower other women to feel more comfortable speaking freely in the future.

NOTE

1. Jane Stevenson and Dan Kaplan, "Women C-Suite Ranks Nudge Up—a Tad," *Week in Leadership*, Women in Leadership Insights, Korn Ferry, 2019, https://www.kornferry.com/insights/this -week-in-leadership/women-in-leadership-2019-statistics.

Adapted from content posted on hbr.org, February 24, 2020 (product #H059K7).

Section 2

BRIDGING GENERATIONAL DIVIDES

7

IS GENERATIONAL PREJUDICE SEEPING INTO YOUR WORKPLACE?

by Kristi DePaul and Vasundhara Sawhney

The year is 2005. YouTube has just launched, and social media usage is on the rise. Mariah Carey and Gwen Stefani are vying for the top song of the year. The first cohort of Millennials is stepping into the workforce. And the business world has plenty to celebrate: The economy is booming, job offers are plentiful and competitive, and technology is advancing faster than ever.

It sounds like a youthful happily ever after. But there was a plot twist: Millennials were eyed warily by their employers and colleagues.

Report after report emphasized how much Baby Boomers and Gen Xers needed to change to accommodate this new generation of lazy, entitled, and disloyal workers and how these young folks would disrupt the workplace as we knew it. The media latched on to these generalizations, reporting that Millennials wanted more "me" time on the job, only took "yes" for an answer, and let their parents assume a peculiarly active role in their professional lives.

As a result, company leaders and senior employees did change, creating processes and policies based on these beliefs. Ping-Pong tables and beer on tap became priorities, constant feedback the gold standard, work-life balance more important than meaningful career progression.

Did these changes actually help Millennials succeed at work? Hardly. While some companies reported lower turnover rates after introducing flexible work schedules, aggressive engagement policies, and wellness programs, the "me me me" generation was actually burning out. Turns out it was filled with workaholics; many discontented Millennials embraced side hustles amid the burgeoning gig economy and the uncertainty of the Covid-19 pandemic. (And no, those Ping-Pong tables weren't necessary.)

As Millennials ourselves, we have been subjected to pervasive stereotyping ("I'm sure you prefer Slack over email") and condescending assumptions ("You've been here for two years. Time to move on?"). If you're part of this generation, you've probably experienced bias like this too. Workers of all generations have—when it comes to our supposed differences from each other, there are plenty of stereotypes to go around.

This made us wonder: Does intergenerational anxiety stem from *actual* differences? Or is it created by the mere *belief* that certain disparities exist? And if it's the latter, what can we do to thwart those stereotypes before we create mismatched workplaces for generations to come?

Why Generational Biases Exist at Work

Beliefs about generations have long provided a flawed but convenient framework for managerial thinking and decision-making. Our research for this article uncovered a few reasons they persist.

We put things in buckets to make sense of them

According to Michael Kramer, former chair of the department of communication at the University of Oklahoma,

"Humans naturally seek simplified explanations for their own and others' behavior through a process of sensemaking, especially during uncertain times. Constructing and adopting stereotypes is one way of doing that."

Bobby Duffy, a professor and the author of *The Generation Myth: Why When You're Born Matters Less Than You Think*, agrees. "We like stories about who we are and who we're not, and we like to categorize everything into what it is and what it's not," he told us. These stories are appealing, especially when they're vivid and memorable, with labels and anecdotes behind them. "And that's certainly what's happened with generational labels," he added.

All of this can make us feel closer to colleagues of our generation. "We feel that when we are born matters because there is a sense of connection to our peers . . . They have gone through what we have gone through. It feels intuitive. And it works really well as shorthand communication in headlines or when we want to sum up complex things in simple labels," Duffy said.

Managers who are nervous or unsure about leading a new age cohort—particularly when the media is putting them on high alert—may rely on generational labels as shortcuts for engaging and attracting those workers. Duffy noted that leaders sometimes use stereotypes as scapegoats when something isn't working. "When you believe that it's not your fault as an employer—that it's just this weird generation coming into the workforce and placing unreasonable demands on you—you shift the blame onto them" instead of understanding and addressing the root issue.

Rosy retrospection plagues us

Cognitive psychologist Gordon Bower found that our memories are reconstructed when we recall them—a process prone to manipulation and errors. Various types of memory bias can affect our decision-making in both positive and negative ways. "Rosy retrospection," or declinism, is one such bias: It refers to our tendency to minimize the negatives of the past, leading us to view it more positively than the present.

Duffy says that, as a result, we think things used to be better than they are now and believe everything is going downhill. "Coupled with generational thinking, we feel the current situation is dreadful; clearly, the new generation is at fault and will change everything," he explained wryly. When we look for someone to blame, a new cohort could, conveniently, fit the bill.

But if you feel that young workers today are being too demanding (whether about wanting better tech infrastructure or sporting tattoos and beards at work), you're probably forgetting that you, too, were insistent and intent on forging your identity at that age. Or as former HBR editor Andrea Ovans put it, "The hippies of the late 1960s became the dress-for-success yuppies of the 1980s."[1]

Employers are vying for talent in any way they can

Consider Google, with its nap pods, on-site laundry service, free snacks, and colorful beanbag chairs. What began as a data-driven recruitment and retention strategy—projecting the company's "cool quotient" to encourage a robust applicant pool and lengthier employee tenures—soon became an industry benchmark that others measured branding efforts against.

More recently, companies have used popular insights to "seem less square." They're marketing themselves as culturally diverse (Millennials expect a diverse workplace), providing collaborative environments (Millennials work better in groups than alone) and flexible work schedules (Gen Zers love work-life balance), and keeping their Instagram profiles up to date (both generations like that one) to attract younger people. Firms are also conducting extensive employer brand surveys to reveal the priorities of specific generations—yet many of the preferred perks identified may not be unique to any age group, like better compensation packages and meaningful work.

Generational stereotypes have created a cottage industry

From books to podcasts to consultancies, there are any number of lucrative reasons to assert that generational differences do, indeed, exist and are central to the workplace. "There's a whole industry around generations," Cort Rudolph, an industrial and organizational psychologist and faculty member at Saint Louis University whose research focuses on work and aging, told us.

Because managers are led to believe they must adapt their approaches for different generations—and are unsure about how to do that—they often seek help that can provide insights and guidance. As a result, "companies go out and hire generational experts to come in and clean up intergenerational conflicts," said Rudolph.

And it's not cheap. As of a few years ago, some consultants were charging $20,000 to $30,000 per hour, and Source Global Research estimated that U.S. organizations spent $60 million to $70 million on generational consulting in 2015 alone. The long-term success of such efforts remains to be seen (we're still debating if Millennials will ever get the workplace they want), but meanwhile generational consulting related to Gen Z has become popular.

Moving Beyond Generational Thinking

But is it really so bad if companies try to leverage popular insights to win over specific generations at work? Well, possibly yes. "We're basing a lot of practice decisions, a lot of policies, a lot of approaches in the workplace on pretty shaky science," Rudolph explained. And it can negatively affect employees. In fact, for this article we posted a LinkedIn poll to ask people if being part of a generation negatively influences how they're treated at work. Sixty percent of respondents said it did.

Often what's happening—which is less intentional than overt ageism—is reflected in organizational practices that, while appearing benign, aren't applied to everyone equally. Rudolph offered an example: the popular narrative that people from younger generations want more flexibility. "As a manager, I'm going to read that and then afford different levels of flexibility to people based on their age. What results is a policy that seems to be grounded in what a certain subset of the population wants—when in reality, *everybody* values flexibility."

Such beliefs can influence everything from how new teammates are onboarded, to how they are trained or mentored, to even how teams collaborate and communicate—and that breadth can pose great risk to organizations' age inclusivity and employee performance. One experiment found that trainers assigned to teach someone a computer-related task had lower expectations and provided worse training when they believed the person was older.

So, how do we design policies and processes that protect us from ageist behaviors, rather than relying on assumptions or stereotypes?

Consider other explanations for employee similarities and differences

"It's really difficult to separate out what is actually a generation from other types of influences that co-occur with time," noted Rudolph. Each of us has more in common with our older and younger counterparts than we might realize, which can be attributed to *life-cycle effects*, or how we grow and change as we age. For example, younger professionals—who are typically less tied down by family obligations—are more likely to experiment with their careers and take risks to find the right fit, as compared with older workers, who are more established in their careers. This is true no matter the generation: A report from the U.S. Bureau of Labor Statistics shows that Boomers did as much job hopping in their twenties as Millennials at that age.

There are other kinds of effects that influence us too. A 2020 report found that people born in the same year or span of years may share some similarities (*cohort effects*), though they may have very different experiences and outlooks depending on social and economic factors or geographic location.[2] People are also influenced by *period effects*, or events and changes (a pandemic, a war, a recession) that impact everyone at a given point in time. Attributing someone's behavior to one effect when it's due more to another effect can lead to misunderstandings.

For example, Millennials and Gen Zers are known for the stereotype that they switch jobs quickly. That might seem to be a cohort effect—young people today like to job hop, perhaps because they're disloyal to employers. But consider that both generations spent their formative years in a recession—a period effect. Members with access to higher-paying roles and industry connections or with the ability to live in a region with ample job opportunities may be doing fine. But many others haven't accumulated wealth the way their predecessors did and have comparatively sluggish earning trajectories. They've also started fewer businesses due to unfavorable economic conditions. These factors, combined with pension plans becoming outmoded and the fact that significant raises usually don't come from advancing in one's current company, have led many younger workers to job hop to seek higher wages—so they can devote more to retirement savings.

Recognize that employees' needs are often universal

Jessica Kriegel, a workplace culture expert and the author of *Unfairly Labeled: How Your Workplace Can Benefit from Ditching Generational Stereotypes*, described to us a town hall meeting gone awry when a CEO stated that Millennials value work-life balance more than compensation. What he believed to be an innocuous comment—a compliment, even—caused an uproar. Employees of all ages complained to HR.

"Millennials were adamant that salary mattered to them and were concerned the organization had offered them less as a result of this work-life belief," Kriegel explained. "And older employees insisted that work-life balance was important to them as well. People generally have a negative reaction to being told who they are and what they value."

So, if managers and leaders should stop using generations as a framework for customizing policies, what should they use instead? Rudolph suggests focusing on actual, identifiable, and relevant differences by adopting a life-span perspective on aging at work—that is, focusing on the differences between and changes within employees as they age.

For example, you might base your policies on the assumption that only Millennials care about work-life balance, autonomy, or flexible working hours. But when you consider a life-span perspective, you realize that any caregiver would find those policies attractive, irrespective of generation. Offering tailor-made policies isn't just an inefficient use of resources, as some employees may not want them; it also ties up resources that would be highly valued by those who actually need them.

Consider societal changes when crafting policies

Task- or work-environment-related changes must address larger societal trends and universal factors, such as pay transparency (employees want to lessen the gender pay gap) or better work-life integration (work isn't the only thing employees want to do with their time).

For example, many couples are choosing to delay having children or not carry children themselves. In response, Zomato—India's biggest food-delivery app—introduced a 26-week parental leave that applies to all employees, including surrogate or adoptive parents as well as same-sex parents. "The needs of our people are more specific to their life stages and the roles they play at work and at home, as compared to the generation they belong to," Daminee Sawhney, the company's vice president, human resources and operations, explained.

Naturally, such policies shouldn't be created in a vacuum. Zomato considers a combination of its culture and the feedback it receives from employees about what they expect from the organization in the long term. "We don't rely on generational studies or consultants to guide us. Instead, we enable our people to operate from a space of accountability and trust and believe in continually assessing and abandoning practices that no longer serve us as a collective," Sawhney added.

The rise in remote work is another example of a societal change that is valuable irrespective of someone's generation. SAP in India designed its work-from-home policy in 2013 in response to employee proposals. The policy has evolved through the pandemic and has been honed to address the future of work.

"Pledge to Flex is an excellent example of how we have taken perspectives of employees representing various personas on what flexibility and hybrid work meant to them and has stood the test of time," Shraddhanjali Rao, the company's head of HR, told us. "Today, we have a playbook that respects individuality and empowers our employees to choose their way of hybrid working, keeping their teams and business context in mind."

Like the shift to working from home, some societal changes will be easy to identify and difficult to ignore. Others will require paying more attention to how new governmental policies might impact workers in your industry or to what other organizations offer employees, such as fertility benefits or tuition reimbursement. Maintaining an open internal dialogue within company forums can help leaders to further identify the supports that are most valued by their workforce.

The above recommendations may not entirely rid your organization of generational biases. But they can help you understand when focusing on generational differences might not be helpful. Only then can you begin building programs and processes that meaningfully support an age-diverse workforce.

TAKEAWAYS

Beliefs about generations provide a flawed but convenient framework for managerial thinking and decision-making. But generational differences aren't as big as most think, and our beliefs about generational cohorts may be largely borne from stereotypes. Once we understand the history of generational stereotypes at work, who has benefited from them, and why we like to place people into buckets, we can learn to create prejudice-free processes and policies that work for all employees, irrespective of birth year.

✓ **Consider other explanations for employee similarities and differences.** Understand the difference between *cohort effects* and *period effects*. Attributing someone's behavior to one effect when it's due more to another can lead to misunderstandings.

✓ **Recognize that employees' needs are often universal.** Erroneous, generation-based assumptions can lead to creating the wrong policies.

✓ **Consider societal changes when crafting policies.** Task- or work-environment-related changes must address larger societal trends and universal factors, such as the need for pay transparency or better work-life integration.

NOTES

1. Andrea Ovans, "Companies Have Always Struggled to Engage Young People," hbr.org, November 18, 2014, https://hbr.org/2014/11/companies-have-always-struggled-to-engage-young-people.

2. National Academies of Sciences, Engineering, and Medicine, *Are Generational Categories Meaningful Distinctions for Workforce Management?* (Washington, DC: National Academies Press, 2020), https://doi.org/10.17226/25796.

Adapted from content posted on hbr.org, March 8, 2022 (product #H06WE9).

8

BEWARE OF AGE META-STEREOTYPES

by Eden King, Lisa Finkelstein, Courtney
Thomas, and Abby Corrington

T he five-generation workforce has resulted in conversations about how generational differences will impact the functioning of our organizations. After all,
Millennials want to communicate with coworkers only
via text—and Baby Boomers don't text, right? And you
need to attract those techy Millennials with promises
of flexible work schedules, but their older counterparts
all want a traditional workday, correct? Well, actually,
wrong.

Most of the evidence for generational differences in preferences and values suggests that differences between these groups are quite small. In fact, there is a considerable variety of preferences and values *within* any of these groups. For example, a thorough analysis of 20 different studies with nearly 20,000 people revealed small and inconsistent differences in job attitudes when comparing generational groups.[1] It found that, although individual people may experience changes in their needs, interests, preferences, and strengths over the course of their careers, sweeping group differences depending on age or generation alone don't seem to be supported.

So what might really matter at work are not actual differences between generations but people's *beliefs* that these differences exist. These beliefs can get in the way of how people collaborate with their colleagues, and they have troubling implications for how people are managed and trained.

Why Do We Have Inaccurate Beliefs About Age?

An emerging area of research in the field of industrial-organizational psychology considers age-related beliefs from two different but intermingling angles. Work on age stereotypes looks at the content and impact of beliefs about people from a particular age group. A stereotype about young people, for example, might be that they are narcissistic.

A relatively newer concept called "age meta-stereotypes" examines what we *think* others believe about us based on our age group. A young person, then, might worry that other people think they are narcissistic, even if the other people are not actually thinking this. If both of these processes are occurring in an age-diverse work-place at the same time, employees are likely having knee-jerk thoughts about what other people must be like (stereotypes) while simultaneously assuming that the same people are making assumptions about them (meta-stereotypes).

Our research suggests that workplaces are brimming with age-related stereotypes and meta-stereotypes, and that these beliefs are not always accurate or aligned. In one survey of 247 young (18–29), middle-aged (33–50), and older workers (51–84), people described the quali-ties that might be true of people in another age group (their stereotypes).[2] They also described the qualities that other people might have about their own age group (their meta-stereotypes).

The pattern of their responses varied by age group. People's stereotypes of older workers were largely positive and included words like "responsible," "hardworking," and "mature." Yet older workers themselves worried that others might see them as "boring," "stubborn," and "grumpy." The stereotypes of middle-aged workers were largely positive ("ethical"), and they believed the other age groups would see them as positive ("energetic").

Stereotypes about younger workers were somewhat less positive, however, resulting in a wider range of stereotypes from positive ("enthusiastic") to negative ("inexperienced"). Even so, younger workers believed that others would see them in a more negative manner than they actually did ("unmotivated" and "irresponsible"). Broadly, these results demonstrate that older and younger workers believe others view them more negatively than they actually do. These cases confirm that neither age-related stereotypes nor meta-stereotypes are accurate.

How Do Inaccurate Beliefs About Age Affect Our Workplaces?

Despite their inaccuracy, people's beliefs have critical implications for workplace interactions. In one laboratory experiment, we asked undergraduate students to train another person on a computer task using Google's chat function.[3] Another undergraduate was asked to listen to the training and then perform the task. We varied whether each person—the trainer and the trainee—appeared to be old (approximately 53) or young (approximately 23) using photographs and voice-modifying software.

We found that stereotypes about older people's ability to learn new tasks interfered with the training they received. When trainers believed that they were teaching an older person how to do the computer task, they had lower expectations and provided worse training than when they believed they were teaching a young person. These results demonstrate that poorer training is a direct result of age stereotypes. The potential consequences of these findings are alarming, as inferior training can result in reduced learning and ultimately interfere with employees' job performance.

Moreover, people's beliefs about what others think about their age group—their meta-stereotypes—can also interfere with their work behavior. A recently published study examined how people react to meta-stereotypes over the course of a workweek.[4] As expected, sometimes people react with a sense of challenge ("Oh yeah? I'll show them!") and sometimes they report more threat ("Oh no, what if I live up to this negative expectation?").

Importantly, these reactions can also impact interpersonal behaviors at work. Both threats and challenges led to conflict at work (like arguing or not getting along with colleagues) and avoidance behaviors (like keeping to oneself and avoiding interacting with others).

TAKEAWAYS

There's little evidence that people of different generations behave markedly differently at work or want markedly different things. And yet because we have stereotypes about people of different ages—and because we have stereotypes about what we *think* people of different ages believe about us—our ability to collaborate with and learn from colleagues in other generations is negatively affected.

✓ In addition to understanding how stereotypes affect thinking, managers should understand the concept of "age meta-stereotypes"—what people *think* others believe about them based on age groups. Beliefs of both types can get in the way of how people collaborate with their colleagues.

✓ Evidence shows that stereotypes have pernicious effects. One study showed that ageist stereotypes caused trainers to provide inferior teaching to learners.

✓ Ageist meta-stereotypes can interfere with work behavior by heightening senses of threat and challenge at work, leading to more conflicts.

NOTES

1. David P. Costanza et al., "Generational Differences in Work-Related Attitudes: A Meta-Analysis," *Journal of Business Psychology* 27 (2012): 375–394.

2. Lisa M. Finkelstein, Katherine M. Ryan, and Eden B. King, "What Do the Young (Old) People Think of Me? Content and Accuracy of Age-Based Metastereotypes," *European Journal of Work and Organizational Psychology* 22, no. 6 (2013): 633–657.

3. Tracy C. McCausland et al. "The Technological Age: The Effects of Perceived Age in Technology Training," *Journal of Business Psychology* 30 (2015): 693–708.

4. Lisa M. Finkelstein et al., "A Daily Diary Study of Responses to Age Metastereotypes," *Work, Aging, and Retirement* 6, no. 1 (January 2020): 28–45.

Adapted from content posted on hbr.org, August 1, 2019 (product #H052OT).

9

WHAT HAPPENS TO YOUNGER WORKERS WHEN OLDER WORKERS DON'T RETIRE

by Nicola Bianchi, Jin Li, and Michael Powell

F or years in the world of symphony orchestras, available positions for oboe talent were scarce. Young oboists waited for chairs at top orchestras to open up, but many principal oboists who had held their positions for decades simply weren't retiring. It's impossible to know how many younger players gave up, changed professions, or lingered in the lower ranks bitterly for years. In the early 2000s, however, many of the senior oboists began to retire. Those departures freed up spots at the top, which freed up spots below that, and so on. Advancement for oboists was suddenly possible. One promising young oboist described the moment as a "gift from heaven."

The oboists' dilemma is a tidy model for what's beginning to happen more broadly across entire economies, as many workers decide to stay in the workforce past retirement age. These "slot constraints" in organizations hold back high-potential younger workers as older ones stick around and create boom-and-bust cycles of talent demand. The problem can create intergenerational conflict, through what we refer to in our research as "career spillovers."

Intertwined internal and external forces cause spillovers within a firm. Internally, spillovers occur when a firm is limited in its ability to provide advancement opportunities for its employees—what we call "career capacity"—so that one employee's advancement comes at the cost of her coworkers'. This can mean that when older workers delay their retirement, younger workers' career advancement stalls. We have studied these issues in the past, and our current research continues to investigate the quantitative impacts of delayed retirement.

At the same time, external forces—industry conditions and macroeconomic trends—shape a firm's career capacity. When orders aren't coming in, the business can't grow; if the business isn't growing, it can't create career advancement opportunities. This creates a vicious cycle. Since younger firms tend to grow more quickly than mature firms, the spillover effect is felt most deeply in mature firms. The slower-growing firms then lose talent to faster-growing ones where career capacity is less diminished, thus making it even harder for mature firms to compete for new growth.

The changes in public policy and the inexorable demographic data compound the challenge of limited career capacity. At the macroeconomic level, most high-income countries have seen an increase in the median age of their populations, which translates to more older workers. Older employees often occupy higher-level positions in their organizations and tend to have lower turnover rates during their last few years in the workplace. Retirement is taking place later and later, both out of choice and because most countries have increased their retirement age due to budgetary pressures.

When we think about a firm's strategic decisions regarding growth and direction, we typically focus on external factors like business opportunities, rather than considering how an internal force like a firm's career capacity can affect its fortunes. An increasing volume of evidence, however, shows that neglecting career advancement, or being unable to provide it, can lead to employee attrition, especially among high-potential workers. In his 2008 book *Talent on Demand*, Wharton professor Peter Cappelli emphasized that "[f]rustration with advancement opportunities is one of the most important factors pushing individuals to leave for jobs elsewhere."

This frustration can lead to intergenerational conflict. Indeed, a KPMG survey carried out in 2013 found that "46% of people agreed with the proposition that older members of staff should retire so that younger workers could have a genuine chance of promotion."[1] This situation is unfortunate for everyone involved and has only gotten worse over the last few years.

The wicked problem is this: Firms need to expand career capacity in the face of demographics that suggest older workers aren't going anywhere even as younger workers want them to move on. While there are no silver-bullet solutions, our research points to some approaches that may be effective.

Encourage Turnover at the Top

If firms limit the amount of time higher-ranked employees can stay in their positions, advancement is engineered into the firm. An orchestra, for example, might limit the tenure of first oboists to no more than 15 years. Mandatory-retirement policies encourage turnover, as well; in recent years, we've seen increases in forced partner buyouts in law, consulting, and accounting firms as a way to expand career capacity. Other forced-turnover policies such as stack ranking can serve a similar role.

The obvious drawback to these strategies is that they may involve forcing out valuable talent. They have other pitfalls as well. For example, decreased job security through mandatory term limits may make jobs less desirable in the first place; while younger workers want older workers to get out of their way, they likely won't want those same policies applied to their own situation. Stack ranking can undermine incentives employees have to help each other, which is why many prominent firms such as General Electric and Microsoft have stopped using it. And for many years, the uneven application of mandatory-retirement policies gave firms cover to discriminate against older workers, which led several countries to abolish them altogether.

While involuntary departures can be hard on employees, they can be made less painful if firms find ways to facilitate postdeparture careers. If the company can find attractive opportunities elsewhere for workers when they leave—a practice that is common in top management consulting firms such as McKinsey & Company, for example—they can ensure that high-level jobs remain attractive even if they are less secure.

Expand the Hierarchy

Instead of forcing people out of chairs, add more oboists. Expanding career capacity—putting more positions at the top—creates advancement opportunities without losing what's already there.

This may, however, create top-heavy organizations with a new set of problems. A prominent example of this is the "brass creep" phenomenon in the U.S. military, in which the relative number of high-ranking officers spiked at the end of the Cold War. As one article on the phenomenon noted, "In World War II, there were 30 Navy ships for every admiral. Now, the Navy has more admirals than ships." In addition to being expensive, having too many cooks in the kitchen can lead to slower and worse decisions: When everyone is in charge, no one is in charge.

One approach to creating more positions at the top without creating chaos is to set up a job rotation policy whereby workers can take turns being in the leadership position. While this approach may seem unorthodox, it has been pursued by the successful Chinese telecom giant Huawei, where "three deputy chairmen act as the rotating and acting CEO for a tenure of six months."

Plan for Growth

Ideally, firms and industries can create career capacity through growth. Form more orchestras! Peter Drucker's famous case study on Callahan Associates in 1977 described a firm that engineered growth by becoming a chain of chains.[2] It started out as a supermarket chain, then developed a chain of garden centers, then home-service centers, and then greeting card stores. It did so because the CEO, Bill Callahan, "deeply believed that the company had to expand to give people promotion opportunities," and "this meant going purposefully into new businesses every six or seven years."

While this strategy expands career opportunities, it may also mean pursuing unusual or risky opportunities, and it can appear unprofitable to outsiders and investors. If left unchecked or pursued in a reactive manner, it can become a cancer on the organization. Engaging in this type of growth requires thinking carefully about the long-term costs of hiring someone and providing them with a fulfilling and motivating career. This approach may mean forgoing profitable short-run opportunities—a mindset that may have been more palatable when Drucker was writing in the 1970s than it is today. Still, companies pursue growth, and it will be part of any strategy aimed at increasing opportunities. The career capacity challenge could be one way to jolt an old firm into the kind of new thinking it needs in order to grow.

. . .

Running a successful organization requires striking the right balance between taking advantage of external opportunities and managing career opportunities. Our research has shown that in many situations the best way to motivate workers is through career-based incentives. When career opportunities are mismanaged, the performance of the firm suffers both in the short run, because of career spillovers and intergenerational conflicts, and in the long run, because such conflicts may make it difficult for the firm to attract new talent. As we've shown here, there are ways for firms to expand their career capacity and reduce these conflicts, although all of these approaches have costs as well. Firms should compare the costs and benefits and not rely on any single approach. An integrative and thoughtful strategy that combines all of these solutions can be the most effective.

TAKEAWAYS

As many workers decide to stay in the workforce past retirement age, "slot constraints" in organizations hold back high-potential younger workers, sometimes creating intergenerational conflict. In the face of demographic shifts, firms need to expand their "career capacity." A few approaches may be effective, but each comes with pitfalls.

✓ Encourage turnover at the top. If firms limit the amount of time higher-ranked employees can stay in their positions, advancement is engineered into the firm. But this strategy may involve forcing out valuable talent.

✓ Expand the hierarchy. Putting more positions at the top creates advancement opportunities without losing what's already there. This may create top-heavy organizations with a new set of problems.

✓ **Plan for growth.** Ideally, firms and industries can create career capacity through growth. Such a strategy requires thinking carefully about the long-term costs of hiring someone and providing them with a fulfilling and motivating career. But this approach may mean forgoing profitable short-run opportunities.

NOTES

1. Brian Groom, "Young Workers Fear Later Retirement Blocks Career Prospects," *Financial Times*, June 30, 2013.

2. Peter Drucker, *Management Cases*, rev. ed. (New York: Harper Business, 2008).

Adapted from content posted on hbr.org, November 26, 2018 (product #H04MU9).

HOW SHADOW BOARDS BREAK DOWN GENERATIONAL BARRIERS

by Jennifer Jordan and Mahwesh Khan

A shadow board is a group of young nonexecutive employees tapped to work with the executive board on strategic initiatives. It's designed to introduce a company's (typically middle-aged) leadership team to new perspectives and insights, thereby helping to drive strategy. The shadow board might contribute to initiatives as significant as developing a new marketing plan, redesigning a business model, or updating key processes in the organization's value chain. It can also shift corporate culture in two ways: Board members can gain access to new perspectives, and younger employees can experience the inner workings of a board and share what they learn with their peers.

As we welcome Gen Z into the workplace, such initiatives are more important than ever. While the Silent Generation, Baby Boomers, and Millennials are still learning how to work together, the addition of Gen Z has brought different challenges to light. Research reveals that this newest generation of employees has suffered the most from Covid-19 isolation, and many workers have been remotely onboarded to teams they still haven't met in person. Gen Z also cares a lot about diversity and inclusion, having entered the workforce during Black Lives Matter, #MeToo, and gender diversity movements.

Forming a shadow board with representatives from a younger generation or two is an effective way to navigate this shift among employees—and prepare for new customer segments and market dynamics.

What Shadow Boards Contribute

We spent five years studying the shadow boards of more than two dozen organizations across Europe, Asia, Africa, and the United States. These organizations ranged in size from very small (25 employees or fewer) to very large (more than 200,000 employees) and included professional service firms, energy giants, regional banks, and nonprofit organizations. All had formally announced the creation of a shadow board within the previous three to five years.

Through our research, we found that the organizations gained two primary benefits. First, they were better able to test and pilot initiatives that were important to younger employees and customers. Second, they more effectively bridged gaps between workers of different generations, which enhanced respect and understanding across the hierarchy.

Testing ideas

Shadow boards can serve as safe spaces for the sharing and testing of new initiatives before implementing them at scale.

For example, at Mövenpick Hotels & Resorts, the executive team had been discussing the need to create a booking app for more than a year. All of the company's competitors had such apps, so it seemed like a no-brainer to develop and roll one out. The IT department conducted extensive feasibility studies, but just as the company was preparing to look for vendors, management ran the idea by the shadow board—and members balked. "Why would you waste your time and money making an app?" they said, explaining that no one wanted to download another app or remember another password. The senior management, IT, and commercial teams considered this view and worked with the shadow board to develop a direct web interface instead. "It was a very cool moment," recalled Craig Cochrane, senior vice president of talent and culture. "I don't know how much time or money we would have spent had it not been for the shadow board giving us that feedback so bluntly."

We spoke to several executives in other companies who agreed that testing ideas with their shadow boards allowed them to stay connected to the changing expectations of younger demographics and empowered them to pursue bolder strategies.

Bridging gaps

Shadow boards give both senior executives and rising young talent regular opportunities to communicate with one another, fostering understanding at both levels. The younger, less-experienced employees learn the complexities of the business, see how leaders make decisions, and get advice on their goals. The senior executives get new information and insights from different parts of the company and form personal relationships with up-and-comers in the pipeline.

At TotalEnergies, the shadow board is made up of a group of employees under age 35. One member describes the experience as a win-win that builds empathy between generations. "Sitting next to the executives and seeing how complicated it is to make decisions for large groups of stakeholders makes us more aware of the realities of leadership," he explained. "And it's beneficial for management since we introduce topics that they might not be aware of yet."

The executive sponsor for the board, Gautier Baudot, echoes those sentiments. "At a critical time in our industry, the shadow board provides insights about how the next generation sees the future of the profession, and we get to know the rising talent," he said. In addition, "we're able to provide learning opportunities to the members of the shadow board."

Forming a Shadow Board

If you think your company could benefit from a shadow board, here are four steps you can take to form one.

Step 1: Define your generational target

Which generation or generations do you want advice from? If your goal is to understand the views of your youngest consumers and employees, look to Gen Z. But if it's to redesign business models or rethink the organizational structure, you might want to look to Millennials.

Step 2: Recruit a diverse group

Once you define your target generation, bring in people who represent different genders, races, functions, cultures, and other types of backgrounds.

Some companies choose candidates from their formal leadership development pools. Others have an open application process for all employees in the selected generations. We recommend the latter approach since it creates more enthusiasm around the shadow board, typically generates a more diverse pool of applicants, helps to uncover hidden talent, and makes employees feel better represented even if they aren't selected. Some organizations combine both strategies, asking designated high potentials to apply and bringing them together with employees nominated by managers.

As far as size, the number of people on your shadow board should match, as closely as possible, the number who sit on the executive board. Having a fairly proportional representation allows for an equal balance of voices on both sides, as well as the opportunity for the shadow board to understand what it "feels" like to be on a board the size of the executive committee. Avoid creating a group that is significantly larger, as complexity of decision-making grows exponentially with the addition of people in a team.

Step 3: Define the time commitment

Across the organizations we studied, members of shadow boards were expected to add the role to their regular responsibilities without extra compensation. By maintaining those dual roles, they were able to keep tabs on what was happening on the ground, report back to and hear from senior leaders and fellow board members, and take the insights and ideas discussed into their day jobs.

But candidates should understand up front that being on the shadow board is a big commitment. Organizations must be clear on how much time someone is expected to contribute and ensure that the tasks assigned don't cause anyone to exceed that amount. We recommend recruiting people with the self-discipline to balance both roles and a true desire to participate. That's why we endorse the standard policy of not paying people for shadow board work: While the evidence is mixed, financial remuneration could create a perverse incentive, overshadowing young employees' intrinsic motivations to contribute to the strategic direction of the organization.[1] In addition, we think it's important that shadow boards not create a financial burden for companies, which is why the decision of whether to start one should be purely about the value the group could bring, rather than about budgetary concerns.

Step 4: Embed the board into organizational decision-making

For a shadow board to have impact, it needs concerted, focused, and deliberate coordination by its sponsors.

One of the biggest mistakes we came across in our research was failing to onboard members and guide their interactions with the executive board in a structured way. The two groups comprise less- and more-experienced people, respectively, from two different levels and generations, so it will take some work to ensure that they can communicate effectively and cooperate. We recommend a formal onboarding period for both boards.

For example, Shakespeare Martineau, a U.K.-based law firm, set aside several days for an offsite where shadow and executive board members got to know one another and devised their governance guidelines. The CEO, Sarah Walker-Smith, explained that her team did preparatory work ahead of time, giving assignments to participants to demonstrate that everyone's voices would carry equal weight at the onboarding sessions. She noted that some executive board members were initially apprehensive, feeling their authority could be undermined. But ultimately, "the prework created common ground and established informal rules of engagement between the shadow and main board, which enabled the retreat to be a resounding success."

After the induction period, the two boards should meet separately and then together to further discuss how they will interact. Important questions to consider include: Will the shadow board be present at every executive board meeting or a subset of them? Will a representative of the shadow board be elected to attend executive team meetings and share the shadow board's viewpoints, then report back to their own board? Will the representative role rotate across the shadow board or be held by one person throughout the board's tenure?

Best practices are to hold several joint board meetings and to have a shadow board representative at some executive meetings. This method allows the shadow board to stay abreast of management decisions while still giving the executive board the autonomy it needs.

Potential Pitfalls

While shadow boards can make lasting contributions to organizations, they can also present challenges. When forming and running a shadow board, be on the lookout for two key pitfalls.

Lack of CEO or executive committee sponsorship

In one company we studied, the shadow board was the brainchild of the CHRO. While she made a convincing argument for why it would benefit the organization, the CEO saw it as a distraction and even a threat. The board lasted one year, and none of its recommendations were taken.

In another case, a shadow board supported by the CEO was formed and just as quickly disassembled because other members of the executive team, who were worried about the company's survival, didn't buy in.

To avoid this pitfall, you need to establish a clear business case for the shadow board that resonates with all stakeholders. The key sponsor must also show their commitment to the board and its success. "I take it seriously, so they take it seriously," Mgcinisihlalo Jordan, the deputy CEO of Deloitte Africa, told us. Publicly celebrating some early wins, like finalizing a deliverable or making a strategic choice, can help to support the business case and manage expectations about the value the shadow board is expected to bring and the timeline it should happen on.

No clarity or purpose

A second major pitfall is a lack of clearly defined output or deliverables. Without such deliverables, shadow boards can be perceived as just another top-management initiative meant for show rather than for substantial strategic or cultural contribution.

Specifically, these can include projects or specific assignments and mandates. For example, at TotalEnergies the shadow board is tasked with learning what the next generation thinks about careers in energy exploration. A regional bank assigned its shadow board to find methods for attracting and retaining the young customers who were flocking to fintechs. It's not enough to merely ask for opinions from your shadow board. You need to know what the organization will do with them.

. . .

Shadow boards are an effective way to break down generational barriers, build trust, and bring diverse groups together to solve problems and respond to fast-evolving market dynamics. When done correctly, with the right planning and goals from the top, shadow boards can put management's finger on the pulse of the organization while also keeping its eyes on the future.

TAKEAWAYS

Shadow boards are groups of nonexecutive employees who work with senior executives on strategic initiatives. They are designed to leverage insights from younger generations and to diversify the perspectives that executives are exposed to. Shadow boards allow younger, less-experienced employees to learn the complexities of the business, see how leaders make decisions, and get advice on their goals.

✓ These boards can be used to test and pilot novel initiatives that are important to younger employees, bridge generational gaps between workers, and create respect and understanding across the organizational hierarchy.

✓ To form a shadow board, your company should define its generational target, recruit a diverse group of participants, define the time commitment, and embed the board into organizational decision-making.

✓ When forming and running a shadow board, its value can be undermined by a lack of CEO support or executive committee sponsorship or by a lack of clearly defined output and deliverables.

NOTE

1. Jason D. Shaw and Nina Gupta, "Let the Evidence Speak Again! Financial Incentives Are More Effective Than We Thought," *Human Resource Management Journal* 25, no. 3 (July 2015): 281–293.

Adapted from "How Shadow Boards Bridge Generational Divides," on hbr.org, March 8, 2022 (product #H06WE9).

11

BRIDGING GENERATIONAL DIVIDES IN YOUR WORKPLACE

by Debra Sabatini Hennelly and Bradley Schurman

Demographic change is one of the least understood yet profoundly important issues facing organizations today. The "working-age population" in the United States—those from age 16 to 64—is contracting at a pace not experienced since World War II. Unlike that period, there is no "baby boom" behind it, and none is expected in the near future. Generation Z has three million fewer people than the Millennial generation, and Generation Alpha, which follows Gen Z, is expected to be even smaller.

Due largely to early retirements and a caustic mix of ageism and cost-cutting measures, businesses let too many older workers go during the pandemic—and when they left, so did a lot of institutional memory, expertise, and loyalty. Those employers didn't account for the reality that there might be too few younger workers to fill those roles as the pandemic subsided.

With fewer younger workers entering the labor market for at least a generation, employers that don't think beyond today's working-age population will likely struggle to build a reliable workforce that can maintain operational efficiency and effectiveness.

Facing the future

In a survey by the Living, Learning, and Earning Longer Collaborative Initiative, more than eight in 10 global leaders recognized that multigenerational workforces are key to growth, yet less than half of companies include age diversity in their DEI initiatives.[1] Prepandemic employment practices won't take us into the future.

Organizations must reconsider their DEI strategies to meet the demands of a new era if they want to drive operational effectiveness, increase competitiveness, widen their appeal to consumers of all ages and abilities, and build long-term resilience. Here's how leaders can account for the changes—and benefits—that come with an aging workforce to power productivity into the future.

Leverage inclusive design to improve retention

Businesses can support employees past the traditional retirement age by shifting strategies from recruitment to retention. Just a few years ago, this would've been unheard of outside of "super-aged" countries, like Germany and Japan, or in sectors like agriculture or public service.

Retaining older workers increases the diversity of organizations and can improve operational efficiency, enhance innovation, and grow the bottom line. A Gartner study revealed that a highly inclusive environment can improve team performance by up to 30%.[2] Another by McKinsey & Company suggested that companies with the most diversity outperform those with the least by 36% in profitability.[3]

Retention rates can be improved when inclusive design practices are levied across three dimensions: compensation and benefits strategies, working arrangements, and workplace design. The practice of inclusive design considers the full range of human diversity, including age and ability.

Compensation and benefits

The tight labor market and rising inflation are pushing workers to demand better pay and improved benefits. Caregiving leave, retirement savings programs, financial checkups, and lifelong learning and reskilling are attractive to all employees, regardless of age. However, some companies are creating novel support for menopause, grandparents' leave, and sabbaticals in order to reward and retain older talent.

Working arrangements

Flexible work is one way to help employees of all ages. This might include remote or hybrid work, a shortened work week, and variable schedules to meet personal or family needs or accommodate mobility challenges. Employees may also be enticed to stay with phased retirement and job-sharing programs.

These types of working arrangements, which were once the provenance of white-collar office jobs, now have the potential to extend to industrial and service-sector jobs, too. Frontline workers, many of whom are required to be on-site, could be offered compressed schedules and more days off; flextime, where they work a set number of hours and choose their starting and finishing times within agreed-on limits; or both.

Workplace design

Workplace design can impact the retention rates of workers, both positively and negatively. Effective inclusive design need not be a major capital investment (although it can be), but rather can consist of small and inexpensive interventions that flow from insights gathered from surveying and talking to employees of all ages and abilities about their user experiences within the workplace. These interventions can include everything from improved ergonomics (e.g., office chairs) to lighting (e.g., type of lighting and access to natural light). When taken together, these small changes can improve and extend workers' well-being and productivity.

Facilitate multigenerational collaboration and communication

Harnessing the perspectives of employees of differing backgrounds can ignite innovation. As Andrey Khusid, Miro's founder and CEO, noted, "When individuals who entered the workforce before email can collaborate smoothly with those who were raised on memes and selfies, your business can bring more widely appealing products to market, craft compelling marketing campaigns to touch millions, and win love for your brand across the generational spectrum."

Multigenerational collaboration does not occur without some nurturing. Here are seven ways to bridge communication gaps and challenge assumptions:

Encourage nontraditional mentoring

Meaningful one-on-one relationships can build intergenerational awareness and break down misperceptions. The concept of two-way, mutual mentoring expands the benefits of traditional, one-way mentoring relationships, as insights and tips can be shared in both directions. The opportunities for senior employees to gain awareness from junior employees in "reverse mentoring" can also provide powerful experiential learning for the older colleague—and with low risk of embarrassment.

When handled well, these relationships can open minds and communication channels, increase comfort levels with technology, and build inclusive networks.

Focus on common ground to build trust

A common obstacle in team effectiveness is the absence of trust, according to Patrick Lencioni's *The Five Dysfunctions of a Team.* When colleagues are afraid to be vulnerable with one another and are unwilling to admit their mistakes or need for help, competition and intimidation undercut connecting. There are no shortcuts to building trust among generations at work.

Tensions can escalate when people make assumptions and objectify each other. Research has shown that actual differences between generations are not as great as stereotypes might suggest (see chapter 8), while there are wide variances (and intersectionality) within generations. But assumptions can be contagious. Beliefs that age-based generalizations are accurate can impact the way we manage and interact.

We can break through stereotypes by finding commonalities across generations. Create opportunities for colleagues with shared strengths, passions, and life experiences to connect on projects, charitable work, and in social events. Employee resource groups (ERGs)—traditionally created as supportive communities for employees who share common ground—can create cross-generational bonds. AARP developed an Intergenerational ERG Toolkit to help employers enhance age inclusivity.

Build bridges across communication divides

Communication preferences and generational dialects can be major obstacles to collaboration. Core values and codes of conduct can fall short of establishing "rules of engagement" for multigenerational teams when a translator and dictionary might be necessary. The disconnects might be as simple as misunderstandings about vocabulary and emoji use across generations or generational preferences for communicating by email, messaging, telephone, and social media.

By confronting these head-on (with some self-effacing humor), a leader can convene a team discussion about communication, sharing their own vulnerability and mistakes first, and ask for other examples that need clarification. You don't have to look too far to find the training ground for successful multigenerational communication: Ask team members to share some successful examples of dealing with these disconnects among multigenerational family members. The team can set collective ground rules for how they communicate and through what media, as well as agreeing on ways to ask for "translations" to avoid miscommunications.

Promote managers who engage multigenerational teams

Innovation and organizational resilience require leaders who can manage across four or five generations and retain the expertise, experience, and wisdom of older employees. There are several essential attributes in this leadership pipeline:

Extend respect and appreciation for the contributions of older employees

Identify and reward managers who are comfortable hiring and managing employees older than they are. The self-awareness required to engage employees with skills or expertise they lack is a necessary insight for achieving team objectives.

Managers must rethink their "filters" on candidate pools to embrace the demographic shift in the working-age population. Recognize and encourage younger managers who don't write off older candidates as "over-qualified" or question why they would apply for a role that seems to be "beneath" them. They understand that there are many reasons why an older candidate might be applying and can be open to learning what that person might offer the team.

Create psychological safety and encourage candor

As Google learned in its enterprise-wide, two-year work-place study, psychological safety is key to having high-performing teams, reducing turnover, and increasing revenues.[4] Professor Lindy Greer noted about Google's findings, "If you just put people together, they're going to crash and burn unless they have conflict-resolution training, a manager who can coordinate roles, and op-portunities to learn with one another."

When employees of different generations shut down each other's contributions as either outdated or naive, re-sentments grow and trust diminishes. Managers who can reframe generational differences as opportunities for col-lective learning can facilitate respectful debate. By creating psychologically safe team environments, managers can build trust for welcoming broader perspectives, new ideas, and dissenting positions—without judgment—and avoid the inertia of groupthink.

Think outside the box to engage long-tenured employees

Promote managers who think creatively—and beyond age-based generalizations—to be inclusive of long-tenured employees.

Workforce resilience requires making reskilling a strategic priority. Proactive managers who plan for valued employees to develop new expertise or take sabbaticals can reengage and prolong those employees' careers.

Beyond adapting to automation and technological changes, for example, employees in manufacturing and services industries could move into training, safety, or compliance roles that take advantage of their operational experience and reputations with colleagues.

. . .

Given the demographic shifts impacting labor and consumer markets, companies need proactive approaches to retain older workers, which will adapt team dynamics for sustainable growth well into the future. Creating that environment requires mutual respect, age-inclusive designs, and encouraging candor to catalyze the creativity grounded in the team's diverse experiences.

TAKEAWAYS

Due to early retirements and a caustic mix of ageism and cost-cutting measures, businesses let too many older workers go during the pandemic—and when they left, so did a lot of institutional memory, expertise, and loyalty. Organizations must now reconsider their DEI strategies in order to retain older workers. This practice will drive operational effectiveness, increase competitiveness, widen their appeal to consumers of all ages and abilities, and build long-term resilience. They should:

- ✓ **Leverage inclusive design to improve retention.** This will involve novel forms of compensation and benefits for older workers, flexible work arrangements, and workplace redesign.

- ✓ **Facilitate multigenerational collaboration and communication.** Harnessing the perspectives of employees of

differing backgrounds can ignite innovation. Encourage nontraditional mentoring, focus on common ground, build bridges across communication
divides, promote managers who engage multigenerational teams, extend respect to older employees,
and create psychological safety in the workplace.

NOTES

1. "Global Insights on the Multigenerational Workforce,"
AARP International, 2020, https://www.aarpinternational.org
/File%20Library/Future%20of%20Work/2020-Global-Insights
-Multigenerational-Workforce-Infographic.doi.10.26419-2Fres
.00399.002.pdf.

2. John Kostoulas, "Technologies Are Critical for Inclusion in the
Workplace," *Gartner Blog Network* (blog), August 30, 2018, https://
blogs.gartner.com/john-kostoulas/2018/08/30/technologies-critical
-for-inclusion/.

3. Sundiatu Dixon-Fyle et al., "Report: Diversity Wins: How
Inclusion Matters," McKinsey & Company, May 19, 2020, https://
www.mckinsey.com/featured-insights/diversity-and-inclusion
/diversity-wins-how-inclusion-matters.

4. Julia Rozovsky, "The Five Keys to a Successful Google Team,"
re:Work, November 17, 2015, https://rework.withgoogle.com/blog
/five-keys-to-a-successful-google-team/.

Adapted from content posted on hbr.org, January 5, 2023 (product #H07FE2).

About the Contributors

NICOLA BIANCHI is an assistant professor of strategy at the Kellogg School of Management at Northwestern University.

ABBY CORRINGTON is an assistant professor of management at Providence College School of Business. She conducts research on the different ways that people express and remediate discrimination. She has received several grants for her work and has published in the *Journal of Vocational Behavior* and *Equality, Diversity, and Inclusion.*

KRISTI DEPAUL is a content creator whose writing on career navigation and personal branding has appeared in international outlets and has been cited by prominent think tanks and universities. She is the founder and a principal at Nuanced, a thought-leadership firm for executives, and serves as CEO of Founders, a fully remote content agency focused on the future of learning and the future of work. She earned a master's degree from the H. John Heinz III College of Information Systems and Public Policy at Carnegie Mellon University.

JENNY FERNANDEZ is a leadership coach, adviser, and mentor for C-suite women, Latinx, Millennials, and Gen Zers. Jenny brings innovative leadership development strategies to senior leaders and their teams to drive exponential growth by amplifying their creative vision, executive presence, influence, and effectiveness. Jenny spent 20 years building strong marketing strategies and global brands at *Fortune* 500 companies, helping grow, scale, and build markets. She teaches at Columbia Business School and NYU.

LISA FINKELSTEIN is a professor in the social and industrial-organizational psychology area of the psychology department at Northern Illinois University and a fellow of the Society for Industrial and Organizational Psychology. She conducts research on diversity, stereotypes, and stigma at work, including age, disability, body weight, and gender, among others. She also studies mentoring relationships, high-potential designation, and humor at work.

BRANDON FOGEL is a doctoral student at the University of Nebraska–Lincoln. He is a coauthor of *Gentelligence: The Revolutionary Approach to Leading an Intergenerational Workforce.*

MEGAN W. GERHARDT is a professor of management and the director of leadership development at the Farmer School of Business at Miami University, as well as the Robert D. Johnson Codirector of the school's William Isaac and Michael Oxley Center for Business Leadership. She is a coauthor of *Gentelligence: The Revolutionary Approach to Leading an Intergenerational Workforce.*

SARITA GUPTA is a codirector of Caring Across Generations, a national campaign working to transform our systems of care so that all caregivers and families can live and age with dignity. She is also the executive director of Jobs With Justice and a nationally recognized expert on home care and the economic, labor, and political issues affecting working people, particularly women and low-wage workers. As a member of the "sandwich generation," Sarita is grappling with the care issues facing more and more Americans, balancing caring for young children with caring for aging parents.

DEBRA SABATINI HENNELLY advises executives and boards on enhancing organizational resilience by creating cultures of candor, inclusion, integrity, and innovation. She engages teams and leaders directly to identify and address obstacles to psychological safety and ethical decision-making, increasing collaboration, well-being, and productivity.

Debbie also coaches ethics and compliance professionals in effective leadership and personal resilience. Her pragmatic approach is informed by her engineering and legal background and decades of corporate leadership, C-suite, and advisory roles in compliance and ethics, legal, environment and safety, and strategic management. Debbie is an adjunct professor in Fordham University Law School's Program on Corporate Ethics and Compliance, a frequent speaker at professional conferences, and the founder and president of Resiliti.

PAUL IRVING is a senior fellow at the Milken Institute and Distinguished Scholar-in-Residence at the University of Southern California Leonard Davis School of Gerontology.

JENNIFER JORDAN is a social psychologist and a professor of leadership and organizational behavior at IMD. Her research and teaching focuses on the leadership challenges of the digital age.

MAHWESH KHAN is a senior adviser and researcher at IMD and a former corporate governance officer at the International Finance Corporation.

EDEN KING is the Lynette S. Autrey Professor of Industrial-Organizational Psychology at Rice University. She is pursuing a program of research that seeks to guide the equitable and effective management of diverse organizations. She has also partnered with organizations to improve diversity climate, increase fairness in selection systems, and design and implement diversity training programs.

KATHRYN LANDIS is an executive and team coach who helps senior leaders empower and inspire their teams, create a lasting positive impact, and become the best versions of themselves in work and life. She is the founder and CEO of the global coaching and advisory firm Kathryn Landis Consulting, an adjunct professor at New York University, and a former leader at American Express and Automatic Data Processing.

JULIE LEE is a clinical psychologist, the director of technology and mental health for Harvard Alumni for Mental Health, faculty, and a consultant. Her work spans *Fortune* 500 companies, technology startups, and higher-education institutions, including Harvard and Brown University. Julie helps organizations and leaders to create culture and teams that promote wellness, mental health, and full engagement at work. She is an advocate for Gen Z leaders.

JIN LI is a professor of management and strategy and economics at the University of Hong Kong.

JOSEPHINE NACHEMSON-EKWALL is the vice president of independent compliance and risk management at Citi. She is a coauthor of *Gentelligence: The Revolutionary Approach to Leading an Intergenerational Workforce.*

JENEVA PATTERSON is a senior faculty member at the Center for Creative Leadership in Brussels, Belgium.

AI-JEN POO is a codirector of Caring Across Generations and the director of the National Domestic Workers Alliance. She has been organizing immigrant women workers in New York since 1996. She is the author of *The Age of Dignity: Preparing for the Elder Boom in a Changing America* and a 2014 recipient of the MacArthur "Genius" Award.

MICHAEL POWELL is an associate professor of strategy at the Kellogg School of Management at Northwestern University.

VASUNDHARA SAWHNEY is a senior editor at *Harvard Business Review.*

BRADLEY SCHURMAN is the author of *The Super Age* and the founder and CEO of the global research and advisory firm The Super Age. He's an expert on demographic change and how it disrupts social, cultural, political, and economic norms across the United States and around the world. His deep understanding of population shifts, coupled with his grasp of emerging trends, makes him an authoritative voice into our future.

NICOLE D. SMITH is the editorial audience director at *Harvard Business Review.*

COURTNEY THOMAS is a doctoral candidate in the social-industrial/organizational program at Northern Illinois University. She conducts research on person perception related to topics like stereotyping, stigma, and diversity. While her research mainly focuses on the aging component of diversity and inclusion, she also conducts research on other stigmatized identities like disability and obesity.

EMMA WALDMAN is an associate editor at *Harvard Business Review.*

Index

Intergenerational ERG Toolkit, 168
Intergenerational Roundtable activity, 14–17
internships, senior, 53–54
interpersonal behaviors, stereotypes and, 133–134
interpretation, 21
  in Describe-Interpret-Evaluate exercise, 12–13
interviews, stay, 33
Irving, Paul, 39–58
isolation, 81
Italy, 48

Japan, 48
Jenkins, Jo Ann, 49
job changes, 122–123
job satisfaction, 31, 45–46
job security, 73
Johnston, Joy, 89–90
Jordan, Jennifer, 147–159

Kenya, Uhuru Generation, 7
Khan, Mahwesh, 147–159
Khusid, Andrey, 166
King, Eden, 129–135
knowledge
  institutional, 34, 42, 162, 172
  sharing, 4
Korn Ferry, 104

KPMG, 53, 140
Kramer, Michael, 115–116
Kriegel, Jessica, 123
Kuwait, 48

Landis, Kathryn, 69–87
language
  ageist, 34, 37
  generational dialects, 168–169
leaders and leadership
  development for, 32
  menopause and, 103–104
  scapegoating by, 116–117
  shadow boards and, 156–157
learning
  from differences, 36, 170–171
  embracing mutual, 4, 17–20, 21
Lee, Julie, 69–87
Legere, John, 47–48
Lencioni, Patrick, 167
lenses, adjusting your, 12–13, 21
Li, Jin, 137–146
Life Alert, 47
life-cycle effects, 121–122
LinkedIn, 84, 120
Living, Learning, and Earning Longer Collaborative Initiative, 162
L.L. Bean, 92–93
loneliness, 81

Is Your Business Ready for the Future?

If you enjoyed this book and want more on today's pressing business topics, turn to other books in the **Insights You Need** series from *Harvard Business Review*. Featuring HBR's latest thinking on topics critical to your company's success—from Blockchain and Cybersecurity to AI and Agile—each book will help you explore these trends and how they will impact you and your business in the future.